J. M. LeMoine

# Quebec

Its Gates and Environs

J. M. LeMoine

**Quebec**
*Its Gates and Environs*

ISBN/EAN: 9783337181390

Printed in Europe, USA, Canada, Australia, Japan

Cover: Foto ©ninafisch / pixelio.de

More available books at **www.hansebooks.com**

# QUEEN'S BIRTH-DAY, 1880

## QUEBEC,

## ITS GATES AND ENVIRONS.

Something about the Streets, Lanes and Early History of the

## ANCIENT CAPITAL.

BY J. M. LeMOINE.

WITH ILLUSTRATIONS, PLAN OF THE SHAM FIGHT,
&c., &c., &c.

QUEBEC:
PRINTED AT THE "MORNING CHRONICLE" OFFICE

1880.

In view of the large number of visitors which the present celebration of the birth-day of Her Most Gracious Majesty, QUEEN VICTORIA, will attract to the old rock-bound city of Quebec, this pamphlet is issued, in the hope that it will supply a want which strangers have felt for some years past. This little *brochure* is not a mere guide-book filled with ordinary details, but a useful and valuable hand-book, containing interesting historical data about the old and new gates of the city, gossip about the streets and lanes and alleys of the town, annals of the quaint places which abound in and around the Ancient Capital, details and a plan of the sham fight which is to take place on the memorable Plains of Abraham, the scene of the great battle in 1759 between Wolfe and Montcalm, together with a concise history of Spencer Wood, the home of the Lieutenant-Governors of the Province, and other details of interest to the tourist and traveller. This pamphlet fills a unique place in the literature of Canada, and its pages cannot fail to instruct, as well as amuse and entertain, Good wine, it is said, needs no bush. It is scarcely necessary to say anything further in the way of introduction; the pages which follow tell their own story.

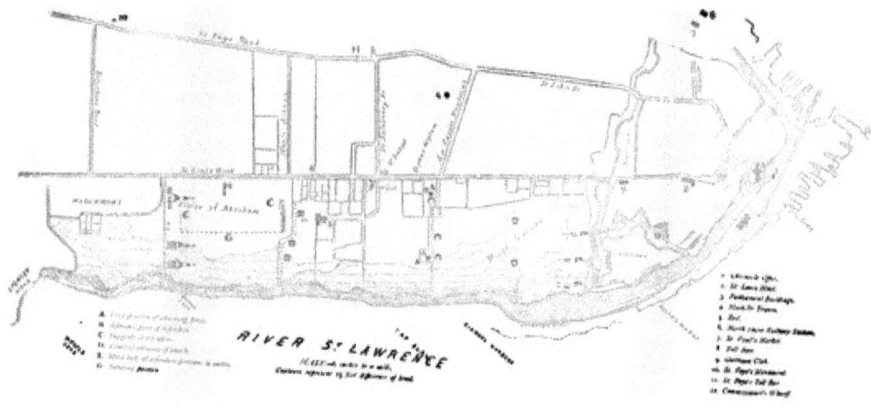

RIVER ST LAWRENCE

# THE REVIEW ON THE QUEEN'S BIRTH-DAY.

The following troops will assemble in Quebec to celebrate the Queen's birth-day :—

|  | Men. |
|---|---|
| "A" and "B" Batteries, 4 guns | 300 |
| The Queen's Own Canadian Hussars, two troops. | 80 |
| Field Battery | 70 |
| 2 Garrison Battery } 3 New Garrison Battery.. } | 200 |
| 8th Infantry | 250 |
| 9th     " | 300 |
|  | 1,200 |
| The Prince of Wales | 250 |
| Victoria Rifles | 325 |
| 5th Fusilier Royal Scots | 275 |
| 6th     " | 275 |
| 65th Battalion | 300 |
| 62nd Battalion (St. John, N. B.) | 275 |
|  | 2,900 |

In all, 2 troops cavalry, 2 field batteries, 5 garrison batteries, 8 infantry battalions.

The corps from a distance will arrive early on Sunday morning, under arrangements made for their transport.

The troops will be drawn up in line upon the Plains of Abraham at half-past eleven o'clock, for which purpose no corps should arrive on the ground later than eleven o'clock. The line will face the St. Louis road, and be drawn up as far back from it as the ground will permit. If there is not space enough for the line the cavalry and artillery on the right will be thrown forward *en potence*.

His Excellency the Governor General and Her Royal
Highness the Princess Louise will, upon arrival, be received
with a Royal salute from the line with colors drooped and
band playing the National Anthem. His Excellency and
Her Royal Highness will probably then ride down the line
and inspect the troops, preceded by the staff in the regu-
lated order of formation. The band of each regiment will
strike up as the procession approaches the right flank of
the corps.

The order will then be given for the troops to load with
blank cartridge. At noon a Royal salute and *feu de joie*
will be fired in honor of Her Majesty's birthday. After
each seven guns the infantry will fire one round of running
fire three times successively. When arms are ordered, the
order will be given "off hats and three cheers for Her
Majesty."

The troops will then march past in column and quarter
column, preparatory to which the infantry will form
quarter column on the right companies of battalions, the
cavalry and artillery conforming.

Immediately after marching past the troops will be formed for the following evolutions of a field day :—

The attacking force will consist of about 1200 men, and
will be formed on the low ground at the extreme edge of
the Plains, close to the Marchmont fence. It will be composed of the following corps under the command of Lieut.-
Colonel Strange, R. A. :—Half troop of cavalry, Quebec
Field Battery, "A" and "B" Batteries (without guns), the
8th Battalion, the 9th Battalion and the 62nd Battalion.
The remainder, with the four guns of "A" and "B" Batteries,
will compose the defending force, and will at once proceed
to take position under the walls of the Citadel, either in the
ditches or the low ground in front of them. They will
throw parties of riflemen into the two Martello towers and

will leave one corps of riflemen under cover of the broken ground near those towers, and another behind Wolfe's monument.

Lieut.-Colonel Duchesnay will command this force. The Western walls of the Citadel will be manned by the five Garrison Batteries of Artillery, and the guns on the bastions commanding the approach from the Plains will have gun detachments told off to each.

Should an attack from the river take place, the guns on the King's Bastion and Eastern face of the Citadel must also be manned.

The troops in the Citadel will be under the command of Lieutenant-Colonel Irwin, R.A.

On a signal being given, the attacking force will advance in order of attack across the Plains of Abraham, they will be first assailed by the outposts near Wolfe's monument, upon which they will open fire and drive them in.

The Martello towers and supporting corps of riflemen, will open fire upon the assailants when within range.

The towers will be captured and the troops driven in, retiring in skirmishing order upon the main body in the Citadel ditches.

The assailants advancing and steadily firing upon the retiring outposts will suddenly be arrested by a fire from the Citadel walls, and simultaneously by a sortie of the infantry concealed in the ditches.

This main body now reinforced by the outposts will advance in order of attack over the cove common and rough ground covered by the fire from the fortress.

They will recover the Martello towers and detach a battalion of infantry supported by cavalry to the right in order to turn the left flank of the retiring force by the St. Louis road, and reach the plains by the gate way near the toll bar.

The retiring force will dispute the ground at every obstacle, especially when there are enclosures and pailings to cover riflemen, but the opposing forces must never approach nearer than 200 yards from each other.

When the retreating force again reaches the open Plains of Abraham assailed on the left flank by the turning movement and in rear by the continually advancing forces, before which they are retiring, they will fight a retreating action till they again reach the point of low ground from which they originally advanced and where they will be lost to sight.

A charge of cavalry might then be made across the Plains in loose order, performing the pursuing practice, with the supposed object of completely dispersing the enemy.

The operations of the troops of all arms when passing and repassing through the enclosed ground, between the new jail and the Martello towers, will require the exercise of the utmost military intelligence and circumspection on the part of the commanders and all the regimental officers and men employed.

Should a demonstration be made by one or more of Her Majesty's ships from the river, I suggest the ships get under weigh in the morning and drop down towards the Island of Orleans. On approaching the city of Quebec about one o'clock, when the land attack on the Citadel would be commencing, they might on hearing the firing from the heights open a broad-side fire for half an hour on the works of the Citadel. This would be hotly returned and at the end of that time they would sheer off with yards canted supposing the lifts and braces to be shot away and with boats hanging disordered in the davits.

The troops after the field day will form a line of quarter columns at close intervals on the original ground, advance in review order, give a Royal salute, and upon the departure of His Excellency the Governor-General and Her Royal Highness the Princess, the Field Artillery will fire a Royal salute of twenty-one guns.

The whole force will be under the command of Lieutenant-General Sir Edward Selby Smyth, K.C.M.G., who will generally direct the evolutions of the troops engaged.

The Scarlet and Rifle Brigades will be commanded by their respective senior officers. The Infantry will be supplied with thirty (30) rounds of blank cartridge per man.

The pouches to be carefully examined to ascertain that no ball cartridge remains previous to the issue of the blank.

The corps proceeding to Quebec should be provided with the full complement of ammunition before leaving their stations.

(Signed,)       E. SELBY SMYTH,
                           Lieut.-General.

Ottawa.

(Certified copy.)

     J. T. DUCHESNAY, Lt.-Col.,
        D. A. G., 7th M. D.

# THE GATES OF QUEBEC.

—— ‡ ——

Of all the historic monuments connecting modern Quebec with its eventful and heroic past, none have deservedly held a higher place in the estimation of the antiquarian, the scholar and the curious stranger than the gates of the renowned fortress. These relics of a by-gone age, with their massive proportions and grim, mediæval architecture, no longer exist, however, to carry the mind back to the days which invest the oldest city in North America with its peculiar interest and attraction. Indeed, nothing now remains to show where they once raised their formidable barriers to the foe, or opened their hospitable portals to friends, but a single substitute of modern construction and a number of yawning apertures in the line of circumvallation that represents the later defences of the place erected under British rule. Of the three gates—St. Louis, St. John and Palace—which originally pierced the fortifications of Quebec under French dominion, the last vestige disappeared many years ago, and the structures with which they were replaced, together with the two additional and similarly guarded openings—Hope and Prescott gates—provided for the public convenience or military requirements by the British Government since the Conquest, have experienced the same fate within the last decade to gratify what are known as modern ideas of progress and improvement—vandalism would, perhaps, be the better term. No desecrating hand, however, can rob those hallowed links, in the chain of recollection, of the glorious memories which cluster around them so thickly. Time and obliteration itself have wrought no diminution of the world's regard for their cherished associations. To each one of them, an undying history attaches and even their vacant sites appeal with mute, but surpassing eloquence to the sympathy, the interest and the veneration of visitors, to whom Quebec will be ever dear, not for what it is, but for what it has been. To the quick comprehension of Lord Dufferin, it remained to note the inestimable value of such heirlooms to the world at large ; to his happy tact we owe the revival of even a local concern for their religious preservation ; and to his fertile mind and æsthetic taste, we are indebted for the conception of the noble scheme of restoration, embellishment and addition in harmony with local requirements and modern notions of progress, which is now being realized to keep their memories intact for succeeding generations and retain for the cradle of New France its unique reputation as the famous walled city of the New World.

ST. LOUIS GATE.

It has more than once been remarked by tourists that, in their peculiar fondness for a religious nomenclature, the early French settlers of Quebec must have exhausted the saintly calendar in adapting names to their public highways, places and institutions. To this pardonable trait in their character, we must unquestionably ascribe the names given to two of the three original gates in their primitive

lines of defence—St. Louis and St. John's gates—names
which they were allowed to retain when the Gallic lilies
paled before the victorious flag of Britain. The erection of
the original St. Louis gate undoubtedly dates back as far
as 1694. Authentic records prove this fact beyond ques-
tion; but it is not quite so clear what part this gate played
in subsequent history down to the time of the Conquest,
though it may be fairly presumed that it rendered important
services in connection especially with the many harassing
attacks of the Iroquois tribes in the constant wars which
were waged in the early days of the infant colony with
those formidable and savage foes of the French. One
thing is certain, however, that it was one of the gates by
which a great portion of Montcalm's army, after its defeat
on the Plains of Abraham, passed into the city on its way
back, via Palace gate and the bridge of boats over the St.
Charles, to the Beauport camp. In 1791, after Quebec had
fallen into British hands, St. Louis gate was reported to be
in a ruinous condition, and it became necessary to raze it to
the ground and rebuild it. Between this date and 1823, it
appears to have undergone several changes; but, in the
latter year, as part of the plan of defence, including the
Citadel, adopted by the Duke of Wellington, and
carried out at an enormous cost by England, it was replaced
by the structure, retaining the same name, which forms the
subject of one of the accompanying illustrations. About
this time seem to have been also constructed the singularly
tortuous outward approaches to this opening in the western
wall of the city, which were eventually so inconvenient to
traffic in peaceful days, of whatever value they might have
been from a military stand-point in trying hours half-a-
century ago. These were also removed with the gate
itself in 1871. On the vacant site of the latter, in accordance with Lord Dufferin's improvement project, a magnificent memorial gate, a sketch of which is shown, and
which the citizens had unanimously agreed to call " The
Dufferin gate," is now in course of erection and will prob-

ably be completed before the close of the present season. The intention of naming it "The Dufferin gate," however, has been abandoned, H. R. H. the Princess Louise, in deference to its traditions and with a graceful appreciation of the feelings of the French element of the population, having recently expressed the desire that it should be allowed

THE NEW (ST. LOUIS GATE.)

to retain its original appellation. Before their departure from Canada, Lord and Lady Dufferin had the pleasure of assisting at the ceremony of laying the corner stone of this new gate, as well as of the new Terrace, which bears their name, and of fairly starting those important works on the high road to realization.

## ST. JOHN'S GATE.

As an interesting link between the present and the past, St. John's gate holds an equally prominent rank and claims an equal antiquity with St. Louis gate. Its erection as one of the original gates of the French fortress dates from the same year and its history is very much the same. Through it another portion of Montcalm's defeated forces found their way behind the shelter of the defences after the fatal day of the Plains of Abraham. Like St. Louis gate, too, it was pulled down on account of its ruinous condition

**OLD ST. JOHN'S GATE (inside) 1864.**

in 1791 and subsequently rebuilt by the British Government in the formshown in the illustration—a form in which it endured until 1865, when it was demolished and replaced, at an expense of some $40,000 to the city, by its present more ornate and convenient substitute, to meet the increased requirements of traffic over the great artery of the upper levels—St. John street. St. John's gate was one of the objective points included in the American plan of assault upon Quebec on the memorable 31st December, 1775; Col. Livingston, with a regiment of insurgent Canadians, and Major Brown, with part of a regiment from Boston, having been detailed to make a false attack upon the walls to the south of it and to set fire to the gate itself with combustibles prepared for that purpose—a scheme in which the assailants were foiled by the depth of snow and other obstacles. This gate, being of quite recent construction and of massive, as well as passably handsome, appearance, is not included in the general scheme of improvement. The erection of a life-size statue of Samuel Champlain, the founder of Quebec, upon its summit, is, however, talked of.

PALACE GATE.

Palace or the Palais gate is the third and last of the old French portals of the city, and derives its title from the fact that the highway which passed through it led to the palace or residence of the Intendants of New France, which has also given its name to the present quarter of the city lying beneath the cliff on the northern face of the fortress, where its crumbling ruins are still visible in the immediate neighborhood of the passenger terminus of the North Shore Railway. Erected under French rule, during which it is believed to have been the most fashionable and the most used, it bade a final farewell to the last of its gallant, but unfortunate French defenders, and to that imperial power which, for more than one hundred and fifty years, had swayed the colonial destinies of the Canadas and contested inch by inch with England, the supremacy of the New World, when a portion of Montcalm's defeated troops passed out beneath its darkening shadows on the fatal 13th September, 1759. After the capitulation of Quebec, General

ARTILLERY STORE—(Palace Gate.)

Murray devoted himself at once to the work of strengthening the defences of the stronghold, and the attention in this respect paid to Palace gate appears to have stood him in good stead during the following year's campaign, when the British invaders, defeated in the battle of St. Foye, were compelled to take shelter behind the walls of the town and sustain a short siege at the hands of the victorious French under de Lévis. In 1791, the old French structure, now a decayed ruin, was razed by the English, but, in the meanwhile, during 1775, it had gallantly withstood the assaults and siege of the American invaders under Montgomery and Benedict Arnold. The somewhat ornate substitute, by which it was replaced and which is shown in the engraving, is said to have resembled one of the gates of Pompeii, and seems to have been erected as late as the year 1830 or 1831, as, in the course of its demolition in 1874, an inscription was laid bare, attesting the fact that at

HOPE GATE.

least the timbers and planking had been put up by local workmen in 1831. It is not intended to rebuild this gate under the Dufferin plan on account of the great volume of traffic, more especially since the completion of the North Shore Railway, to whose terminus the roadway which leads over its site is the most direct route. To mark that memorable spot, however, it is intended to flank it on either side with picturesque Norman turrets rising above the line of the fortification wall, as represented in the illustration.

Hope Gate, also on the northern face of the ramparts, was the first of the two purely British gates of Quebec, and was erected in 1786 by Colonel Henry Hope, Commandant of the Forces and Administrator of the Province, from whom it takes its name. It was demolished in 1874 for no especial reason, this gate being no obstacle whatever to the growing requirements of traffic, as will be readily understood from its situation and the style of its construction as illustrated herewith. Like Palace gate, too, it is

HOPE HILL.

not to be rebuilt—its approaches being easily commanded and its position on the rugged, lofty cliff being naturally very strong. Its site, however, will be marked in the carrying out of the Dufferin Improvements by flanking Norman turrets, as shown in the accompanying engraving.

The last of the city gates proper, wholly of British origin, but the first that grimly confronted in by-gone days the

visitor approaching the city from the water-side and
entering the fortress, is or rather was Prescott gate, which
commanded the steep approach known as Mountain Hill.
This gate, which was more commonly known as the Lower
Town gate, because it led to that part—the oldest—of the
city known by that name, was erected in 1797, (to replace
a rough structure of pickets which existed at this point
from the time of the siege by the Americans in 1775) by
General Robert Prescott, who served in America during
the revolutionary war, and, after further service in the

PRESCOTT GATE.

West Indies, succeeded Lord Dorchester as the British
Governor-General in Lower Canada in 1796, dying in 1815,
at the age of 89 years, and giving his name to this memento
of his administration, as well as to Prescott, Ontario. Old
Prescott gate, an illustration of which is also given, was
unquestionably a great public nuisance in times of peace,
its demolition in 1871 consequently provoked the least
regret of all in connection with the obliteration of those
curious relics of Quebec's historic past. For reasons, which

are obvious, it would be impossible to replace Prescott gate with any structure of a like character, without impeding seriously the flow of traffic by way of such a leading artery as Mountain Hill. It will, however, be replaced by a light and handsome iron bridge of a single

MOUNTAIN HILL—IRON BRIDGE.

span over the roadway with flanking Norman turrets as shown in the engraving.

Our illustrations will be found to also include the representation of another gate marked "Kent gate.' For

the information of our visitors and strangers generally, we
may explain that a few years since the western fortification
wall between St. John's gate and the military exercising
ground in past years, known as the Esplanade, was cut
through to form a roadway communicating between the

KENT GATE.

higher levels of the Upper Town and the St. Louis suburbs,
now styled Montcalm Ward. It consequently became
necessary, in keeping with the æsthetic spirit of the whole
Dufferin scheme, to fill up in some way this unsightly gap
without interfering with the traffic. It was finally decided
to erect here one of the proposed memorial gates, which is

altogether therefore an addition to the number of the existing gates or their intended substitutes. This edifice, which has been commenced and will probably also be finished this season, has been designed to do homage to the memory of Edward, Duke of Kent, the father of Queen Victoria. This gate will be the most imposing of all in the entire circuit of the fortifications, while it has had the signal honor of further being reserved for a handsome subscription towards its cost from Her Majesty's privy purse and dedication at the hands of H. R. H. the Princess, who laid its corner stone with appropriate ceremonial during the month of June, 1879.

### THE CITADEL GATES.

Besides the foregoing, however, the fortress possesses in reality two other gates of much interest to the stranger. When the famous Citadel, commanding the entire harbour and surrounding country, was constructed on Cape Diamond, the number of existing gates was increased from five to seven by the erection of the Chain and Dalhousie or Citadel gates, leading to that great fortilice of British power, which may be aptly styled the *summum opus* of the magnificent but costly system of strategic works that has earned for Quebec its title of the Gibraltar of America. But, as these belong rather to the Citadel, which is an independent stronghold of itself, rather than to the defensive works of the city proper, it suffices to mention that they were erected under the administration of the Earl of Dalhousie, in 1827, and that they are well worthy of a visit of inspection—the one being a handsome and formidable barrier of its class and the other of very massive construction and considerable depth.

Our closing illustration is intended to show the proposed Château St. Louis or Castle of St. Louis, which must be regarded as the crowning feature of the Dufferin scheme of embellishment and was designed by the late Governor

General to serve as a vice-regal residence during the sojourn of the representative of the Crown in Quebec, as well as to revive the historic splendors of the ancient pile of that name, which formed the abode of the early Governors of New France. Of course, this noble structure only exists

THE CASTLE OF ST. LOUIS.

as yet on paper; but, should it ever be erected, it will be a striking object from any point whence the Citadel is visible as it will rise to a considerable height above its highest battlements, standing out in bold relief to the east of the building known as the Officers' Quarters, with a frontage of 200 feet

24

and an elevation partly of 60 and partly of 100 feet, with a basement, two main storeys, and mansard roof and two towers of different heights, but of equally charming design—the style of architecture of the whole being an agreeable *mélange* of the picturesque Norman and Elizabethan.

## SOME OF THE PLACES OF INTEREST

### IN AND ABOUT QUEBEC.

Durham and Dufferin Terraces, 1400 feet long, and 200 feet above and facing the St. Lawrence.

Citadel.

Governor's Garden.

Grand Battery.

French Cathedral.

English Cathedral.

Seminary Chapel (Paintings by Champagne, &c.)

Where Montgomery fell.

Plains of Abraham, and Monument where Wolfe fell at the taking of Quebec, in 1759.

Drive out St. Louis and in through St. Foy's Road.

Falls of St. Ann's.

Falls of Montmorenci.

Indian Village of Lorette and Falls.

Chaudière Falls.

Lakes St. Charles and Beauport abound with Trout and are within two hours' drive of the city.

New Fortifications, Levi.

# OLD AND MODERN QUEBEC.

## Its Streets—Edifices—Monuments—Chronicles—Antiquities, &c.

### By J. M. LeMoine.

On more occasions than one, it has been our pleasant office to escort literary friends round our streets—our ramparts—our battle-fields, occasionally, illustrious visitors ; our accepted task, sometimes an arduous one, consisted in ministering to the craving for historical lore which invariably besets outsiders, once drawn within the magic circle of the associations evoked by the Gibraltar of British America.

It has occurred to us that a mode, as effectual as it seems pleasant, of imparting information would be a survey, minute and methodical, of the *locale*, by us so oft travelled over, jotting down what each street offered worthy of note ; in fine, to treat our valued friends to an antiquarian ramble round the " Old Curiosity Shop." What a field for investigation. Has not each thoroughfare its distinctive feature—its saintly, heathenish, courtly, national, heroic, or burlesque name ? Its peculiar origin ? traceable sometimes to a shadowy—a remote past, sometimes to the utilitarian present. What curious vistas are unfolded in the birth of its edifices—public and private—alive with the memories of their clerical, bellicose, agricultural or mercantile founders ? How much mysterious glamour, is necessarily shed over them by the relentless march of time--by the vicissitudes inherent to human affairs ? The edifices, did

4

we say? Their origin—their progress, their decay, mayhap their demolition by the modern iconoclast—have they no teachings? How many phases in the art of the builder and engineer, from the high-peaked Norman cottage to the ponderous, drowsy Mansard roof—from Champlain's picket fort to the modern citadel of Quebec?

The streets and by-ways of famous old-world cities have found chroniclers—in some instances, of rare ability: Timbs, Howitt, Augustus Sala, Longfellow, &c., why should not those of our own land obtain a passing notice?

Show us on American soil, a single city intersected by such quaint, tortuous, legend-loving streets as old Quebec? Name a town, retaining more unmistakable vestiges of its rude beginnings—of its pristine, narrow, Indian-haunted, forest paths?

In fact, does not history meet you at every turn? Every nook, every lane, every square, nay even the stones and rocks, have a story to tell—a record to unfold—a tale to whisper of savage or civilized warfare—a memento to thrill the patriot—a legend of romance or of death—war, famine, fires, earthquakes, land and snow slides, riot, &c.?

Is it not to be apprehended that in time, the inmates of such a city, might become saturated with the overpowering atmosphere of this romantic past—fall a prey to an over-weening love of old memories—become indifferent, dead-like—to the feelings and requirements of the present? This does not naturally follow. We are, nevertheless, inclined to believe that outward objects may act powerfully on one's inner nature: that the haunts and homes of men, are not entirely foreign to the thoughts, pursuits, impulses, good or bad, of their inmates.

Active—cultured—bustling—progressive citizens, we would fain connect with streets and localities partaking of that character, just as we associate cheerful abodes with sunshine, and repulsive dwellings with dank, perennial shadows.

## CHAP. I.

The Upper Town, in 1608, with its grand oaks, its walnut trees, its majestic elms, when it formed part of the primeval forest, must have been a locality abounding in game. If Champlain, his brother-in-law, Boullé, as well as his other friends of the Lower Town,* had been less eager in hunting other inhabitants of the forest infinitely more dreaded (the *Iroquois*,) instead of simply making mention of the foxes, which prowled about the residency, (*l'Abitation*) they would have noted down some of the hunting raids which were probably made on the wooded declivities of Cape Diamond and in the thickets of the *Coteau Sainte-Geneviève*, more especially when scurvy or the dearth of provisions rendered indispensable, the use of fresh meats. We should have heard of grouse, woodcock, hares, beavers, foxes, *carriboux*, bears, &c., at that period, as the probable denizens of the mounts and rallies of ancient Stadacona.

In 1617, the chase had doubtless to give way to tillage of the soil, when the first resident of the Upper Town, the apothecary Louis Hébert, established there his hearth and home. In that year, " he presently," says Abbé Ferland, "commenced to grub up and clear the ground, on the "site on which the Roman Catholic cathedral and the "Seminary adjoining now stand, and that portion of the "Upper Town which extends from *Ste. Famille Street*, up "to the *Hôtel-Dieu*. He constructed a house and a mill "near that part of St. Joseph street, where it received St. "François and St. Xavier streets. These edifices appear "to have been the first which were erected in the locality,

---

* Up to 1617 and later, Champlain's residence was in the Lower Town and stood nearly on the site of the Church *Notre-Dame des Victoires.*

"now occupied by the Upper Town." At that period, there could have existed none other than narrow paths, irregular avenues following the sinuosities of the forest. In the course of time, these narrow paths became levelled and widened. Champlain and Sir David Kirtk bothered themselves very little with improving highways. Overseers of roads and *Grand-Voyers* were not then dreamed of in *La Nouvelle France :* those blessings, macadamised roads, date from 1841.

One of the first projects of Governor de Montmagny, after having fortified the place, was to prepare a plan for a city, to lay out, widen and straighten the streets, assuredly not without need. Had he further extended this useful reform, our Municipal Council to-day, would have been spared a great amount of vexation, and the public in general, much annoyance. On the 17th November 1623, a roadway, or ascent leading to the Upper Town, had been effected, less dangerous than that which had previously existed. "As late as 1682, as appears by an authentic record (*procès-verbal*) of the conflagration, this hill was but fourteen feet wide. It was built of branches, covered with earth ; rendered unserviceable by the fire, the inhabitants had it widened six feet, as they had to travel three miles, after the conflagration, to enter the Upper Town by another hill."—(T. B. Bedard.)

In the summer season, our forefathers journeyed by water, generally, in birch-bark canoes. In winter, they had recourse to snow shoes.

To what year can we fix the advent of wheeled vehicles ? We have been unable to discover

The first horse consigned to the Governor of the colony, arrived from France, in 1648. Did His Excellency use him as a saddle horse only ? or, on the occasion of a New Year's day, when he went to pay his respects to the Jesuit Fathers, and to the good ladies of the Ursulines to present with the compliments of the season, the usual New Year's gifts † was he driven in a *Cariole* and in a *Calèche*, in the summer season? Here again, is a nut to crack for commentators.

Although there were horned cattle at Quebec, in 1623, oxen for the purpose of ploughing the land, were first used on the 27th April, 1628.

On the 16th of July, 1665, (‡) a French ship brought twelve horses. These were doubtless the mountings of the brilliant staff of the great Marquis de Tracy, Viceroy. These dashing military followers of Colonel de Salières, this *jeunesse dorée* of the Marquis de Tracy, mounted on these twelve French chargers, which the aborigines named "the moose-deer (*orignaux*) of Europe," doubtless cut a great figure at Quebec. Did there exist *Tandems*, driving clubs in 1665? *Quien sabe?* A garrison life in 1665-7, and its amusements must have been much what it was one century later, when the "divine" Emily Montague § was corresponding with her dear "Colonel Rivers," from her Sillery abode, in 1767; she then, amongst the vehicles in use, mentions *Calèches*.

They were not all saints such as Paul Dupuy, (‖) these military swells of Colonel de Salières! Major Lafradière, for instance, might have vied with the most outrageous rake which the *Guards* of Queen Victoria may have numbered in the Colony, two centuries later.

If there were, at Quebec, twelve horses for the use of gentlemen, they were doubtless not suffered to remain idle in their stable; the rugged paths of the Upper Town

† Those gifts consisted of wine (Spanish), meat pies (*tourtières*), capons, books of devotion, etc.—(See *Jesuits' Journal*.)

‡ Histoire de la Colonie Française en Canada. Vol. III., p. 354.

§ History of Emily Montague, 4 Vols., 1767—London.

‖ Histoire de l'Hôtel-Dieu de Québec, (Mère Juchereau, 511.)

were levelled and widened; the public highway ceased being reserved for pedestrians only. This is what we wanted to arrive at.

In reality, the streets of Quebec grew rapidly into importance in 1665. Improvements effected during the administration of the Chevalier de Montmagny, had been much appreciated. The illustrious Chevalier had his *Saint Louis, Saint Anne, Richelieu, D'Aiguillon, St. John streets*, to do honor to his Master, Louis XIII, his Queen, the beautiful Anne of Austria; the Cardinal of Richelieu; his niece, la Duchesse D'Aiguillon; the good priest, St. Sauveur.

In the last and in the present century, St. Louis street was inhabited by many eminent persons. Chief Justice Sewell resided in the stately old mansion, now occupied as the Lieutenant-Governor's offices; this eminent jurist died in 1839. "One bright, frosty evening of January, 1832," says Mr. Chauveau, "at the close of a numerously attended public meeting held at the Ottawa Hotel, to protest against the arrest of Messrs. Tracy, Editor of the *Vindicator*, and Duvernay, Editor of the *Minerve*, the good citizens of Quebec, usually so pacific, rushed, in a noisy procession, led by a dozen students wearing tri-color ribbons, in their button-holes, and sang the *Marseillaise* and the *Parisienne*, under the windows of the Chief Justice, whose ear was little accustomed to such a concert." The ermined sage, 'tis said, was so startled, that he made sure a revolution was breaking out.

" Among the fiery, youthful leaders, the loudest in their patriotic outburst, there was one, who would then have been much surprised had any one predicted that after being President of the Legislative Council—Prime Minister of the Canadas—Knighted by H. R. H. the Prince of Wales in person, he would one day, as Lieutenant-Governor, enter in state this same former residence of Chief Justice Sewell, whilst the cannon of Britain would roar a welcome—the flag of England stream over his head and a British regiment present arms to him." Such, however, has been the fate of Sir Narcissus Fortunatus Belleau.

The mansion of Mr. de Lotbinière, in St. Louis street, was the residence of the *chère amie* of M. Bigot, (the *Intendant*), Madame Pean ; the late Judge Elmsley resided there about the year 1813 ; Government subsequently purchased it to serve as an Officers' Barracks. Nearly opposite the old Court House, (burned in 1872), stands the "Kent House," in which His Royal Highness, the late Duke of Kent resided in summer, 1791-3. (§) No. 42 St. Louis street, is the house† which belonged to the cooper, François Gobert ; it now has become historical. In it were deposited the remains of General Montgomery, on the 31st December, 1775. This summer it is leased by Louis Gonzague Baillargé, Esq., the proprietor, to Widow Pigott, whose late husband was in the "B" Battery.

In the street sacred to Louis XIII, St. Louis street, Messrs. Brown* & Gilmor, established in 1764,‡ their printing office for the *Quebec Gazette*, "two doors higher up than the Secretary's Office," wherever this latter may have stood. The *Gazette* office was subsequently removed to Parloir Street, and eventually settled down for many a long year, at the corner of Mountain Hill, half way up, facing *Break Neck* steps—the house was, with many others removed in 1850, to widen Mountain Street. According

---

(§) " To Let.—That elegant house, No. 6 Port Louis St., lately occupied by H. R. H. Prince Edward and at present by the Lord Bishop of Quebec. For particulars, apply to Miss Mahane, or to Munro & Bell, Quebec.—4th March, 1794. (Quebec *Gazette*—1794.)

† Montgomery's House is now a much frequented stand for the sale of Cigars, Candies, Newspapers, &c., to tourists.

* William Brown, uncle to the Nelsons, was a Scotchman from Philadelphia, who had been induced to print a journal in Quebec from the representations and information he had collected from William Laing, a Quebec Merchant-Tailor, whom he had met in Scotland.

‡ Twenty-four years in advance of the *London Times*, founded in 1788.

to a tradition published in the *Gazette* of 2nd May, 1848, the prospectus of this journal had, it would appear, been printed, in Benjamin Franklin's printing office.

The Abbé Vignal resided at the corner of this and Parloir street, previous to joining the *Sulpiciens;* in 1661, he was roasted alive and eaten by the Indians at *Prairie de la Magdeleine,* near Montreal. In our day, the judicial and parliamentary heads, and the Bar have monopolized it. In it, we find Sir N. F. Belleau, Chief Justice Duval, the Judges Taschereau, Tessier, Bossé, Caron, Routhier ; Hon. L. H. Langevin, P. Pelletier, M. P. ; Messrs. Bossé, Baby, Alleyn, Languedoc, Tessier, Chouinard, Hamel, Gauthier, Bradley, Dunbar, *cum multis aliis,* many of whose clients are as early birds as those in the days of Horace.

"Sub cantu Galli."

"On ascending," says Abbé Faillon, "from the Lower to the Upper Town by a tortuous road, contrived betwixt the rocks, and on the right hand side, we reach the Cemetery.* This road, which terminated at the Parish Church, divided itself into two,—on one side it led to the Jesuits (Jesuits' College) and to the Hospital (Hôtel Dieu,)—and on the other, to the Indian Fort (¶) and to the Castle of Saint Louis. The Castle and King's Fort, guarded by soldiers night and day, under the orders of the Governor, was of an irregular shape, flanked by bastions, fortified by pieces of artillery and contained in its interior several *suites* of apartments separated one from the other. At the distance of about forty toises (240 feet,) from the Castle was seen, on the south side, a small garden fenced-in, for the use of the Governor, and in front, towards the west, was the *Place d'Armes,* (now the *Ring,*) in the form of a trapezium.

---

* Opposite to Mr. Narcisse Turcotte, Jeweller, on Mountain Hill.

¶ The Indian Fort (*Fort des Hurons*) was built to protect the unfortunate Hurons who, after the butchery of 1648-49, had sought refuge at Quebec. It is conspicuous on an old plan of Quebec of 1664, republished by Abbé Faillon. It stood on the northern slope of Dufferin Terrace, on the site to the east of the present Post-Office.

Professor Kalm's description of the public edifices, in 1749, is worthy of note.

"The Palace (Château Saint Louis) is situated on the west or steepest side of the mountain, just above the lower city. It is not properly a palace, but a large building of stone, two stories high, extending north and south. On the west side of it is a court-yard, surrounded partly with a wall, and partly with houses. On the east side, or towards the river, is a gallery as long as the whole building, and about two fathoms broad, paved with smooth flags, and included on the outside by iron rails, from whence the city and the river exhibit a charming prospect. This gallery serves as a very agreeable walk after dinner, and those who come to speak with the governor-general wait here till he is at leisure. The palace is the lodging of the governor-general of Canada, and a number of soldiers mount the guard before it, both at the gate and in the court-yard ; and when the governor, or the bishop, comes in or goes out, they must all appear in arms and beat the drum. The governor-general has his own chapel where he hears prayers; however, he often goes to Mass at the church of the *Récollets*, which is very near the palace."

The Castle St. Lewis, built by Champlain, in 1624, was much improved and enlarged by the wing still existing, erected in 1784 by Governor Haldimand. The old *Château* was destroyed by fire on 23rd January, 1834. On its lofty site and far beyond, is perched our incomparable, world-renowned *Boulevard*: the Dufferin Terrace.

"The Jesuits' Church is built in the form of a cross, and has a round steeple. This is the only church that has a clock............ ....................... .............................."

This little church, of which the corner stone was laid by the Governor General, the Marquis de Tracy, on 31st May, 1666, existed until 1807. The oldest inhabitant can yet recall, from memory, the spot where it stood, even if we had not the excellent drawing made of it with a dozen of other Quebec views—by an officer in Wolfe's fleet, Captain Richard Short. It stood on the site recently occupied by the shambles, in the Upper Town, facing the Clarendon Hotel. Captain Short's pencil bears again testimony to the exactitude, even in minute things, of Kalm's descriptions : his Quebec horses, harnessed one before the other to carts. You see in front of the church, in Captain Short's sketch, three good sized horses drawing a heavily laden two wheeled cart, harnessed one before the other. The church was also used until 1807 as a place of worship for Protestants. Be careful not to confound the Jesuits' Church with the small chapel in the interior of their college (the old Jesuit Barracks) contiguous thereto. This latter chapel had been commenced on the 11th July, 1650, The Seminary Chapel, and Ursulines Church, after the destruction by shot and shell, in 1759, of the large R. C. Cathedral, were used for a time as parish churches. From beneath the chief altar of the Jesuits' Church was removed, on the 14th May, 1807, the small leaden box containing the heart of the founder of the Ursulines' Convent, Madame de la Peltrie, previously deposited there in accordance with the terms of her Last Will.

You can see, that the pick-axe and mattock of the "*bande noire*" who robbed our city walls of their stones, and demolished the Jesuits' College and city gates, were busily employed long before 1871.

There are few, we will venture to say, who, in their daily walk up or down Fabrique Street, do not miss this hoary and familiar land mark, the Jesuits' College. When its removal was recently decreed, for a long time it resisted the united assaults of hammer and pick-axe, and yielded, finally, to the terrific power of dynamite alone.

The Jesuits' College, older than Harvard College, at Boston, takes one back to the dawn of Canadian history.

Though a considerable sum had been granted to foster Jesuit establishments at Quebec, by a young French noblemau, René de Rohault, son of the Marquis de Gamache, as early as 1626, it was on the 18th March, 1637, only, that the ground to build on, "twelve arpents of land, in the vicinity of Fort St. Louis : " were granted to the Jesuit Fathers. In the early times, we find this famous seat of learning playing a prominent part in all public pageants ; its annual examinations and distribution of prizes called together the *élite* of Quebec society. The leading pupils had, in poetry and in verse, congratulated Governor d'Argenson on his arrival in 1658. On the second July, 1666, a public examination on logic brought out with great advantage two most promising youths, the famous Louis Jolliet, who later on joined Father Marquette in his discovery of the Mississippi, and a Three Rivers youth, Pierre de Francheville, who intended to enter Holy Orders. The learned Intendant Talon was an examiner; he was remarked for the erudition his latin questions displayed. Memory reverts to the times when the illustrious Bossuet was undergoing his latin examinations at Navarre, with the Great Condé as his examiner; France's first sacred orator confronted by her most illustrious general.

How many thrilling memories were recalled by this grim old structure? Under its venerable roof, oft' had met, the pioneer missionaries of New France, the band of martyrs, the geographers, discoverers, *savants* and historians of this learned order : Dolbeau, de Quen, Druillettes, Daniel, de la Brosse, de Crepieul, de Carheil, Brebœuf, Lallemant, Jogues, de Noue, Raimbeault, Albanel, Chaumonot, Dablon, Ménard, LeJeune, Masse, Vimont, Ragueneau, Charlevoix, * and crowds of others. Here, they assembled to receive their orders, to compare notes, mayhap, to discuss the news of the death or of the success

---

* Faucher de Saint Maurice*

of some of their indefatigable explorers of the great West ; how the "good word" had been fearlessly carried to the distant shores of lake Huron, to the *bayous* and perfumed groves of Florida, or to the trackless and frozen regions of Hudson's Bay.

Later on, when France had suppressed the order of the Jesuits, and when her lily banner had disappeared from our midst, the college and its grounds were appropriated to other uses—alas ! less congenial.

The roll of the English drum and the sharp "word of command" of a British adjutant or of his drill sergeant, for a century or more, resounded in the halls, in which latin orisons were formerly sung ; and in the classic grounds, and grassy court, * canopied by those stately oaks and elms, which our sires yet remember—to which the good Fathers retreated in sweet seclusion, to "say" their *Breviaries* and tell their beads, might have been heard the coarse joke of the guard room and coarser oath of the trooper.

It had been claimed as a "magazine for the army contractor's provisions on 14th November, 1760." On the 4th June, 1765, His Excellency General James Murray had it surveyed and appropriated for quarters and barracks for the troops, all excepted some apartments ; the court and garden was used as a drill and parade ground until the departure of Albion's soldiers.

How singular, how sad to think that this loved, this glorious relic of the French *régime*, entire even to the Jesuit College arms, carved in stone over its chief entrance, should have remained sacred and intact during the century of occupation by English soldiery—and that its destruction should have been decreed so soon as the British legions, by

---

* A memorable Indian Council was held in the court of the Jesuits' College, on 31st August, 1666.

their departure, in 1871, had virtually handed it over to the French Province of Quebec?

The discovery on the 28th August, 1878, of human remains beneath the floor of this building—presumed to be those of some of the early missionaries—induced the authorities to institute a careful search during its demolition. These bones and others exhumed on the 31st August, and on the 1st and 9th September, 1878, were pronounced by two members of the faculty, Drs. Hubert Larue and Chs. E. Lemieux, both Professors of the Laval University, (who signed a certificate to that effect) to be the remains of three* persons of the male sex and of three † persons of the female sex. Some silver and copper coins were also found, which with these mouldering remains of humanity, were deposited

---

* Mr. Faucher de Saint Maurice having been, in 1878, charged by the Premier, Hon. Mr. Joly, to watch the excavations and note the discoveries, in a luminous report, sums up the whole case. From this document, among other things, wo glean that the remains of the three persons of male sex are those of :

1° Père François du Péron, who died at Fort St. Lonys, (Chambly) 10th November, 1665, and was conveyed to Quebec for burial.

2° Père Jean de Queo, the discoverer of Lake Saint John, who died at Quebec, on 8th October, 1659, from the effects of a fever contracted in attending on some of the passengers brought here that summer by the French ship *Saint André*.

3° Frère Jean Liegeois, scalped 29th May, 1655, by the Agniers at Sillery—(the historian Ferland assigns as the probable spot, the land on which the late Lieutenant Governor Caron built his Mansion "Clermont," now occupied by Thomas Beckett, Esquire.) The remains of this missionary, when excavated, were headless—which exactly agrees with the entry in the *Jesuits' Journal*, May, 1655, which states that Jean Liegeois was scalped—his head cut off and left at Sillery, while his mutilated body, discovered the next day by the Algonquins, the allies of the French, was brought to Sillery, (probably to the Jesuits' residence, the same solid old structure close to the foundations of the Jesuits' chapel and monument at the foot of the Sillery Hill, which many here have seen), from whence it was conveyed to the Lower Town in a boat and escorted to the Jesuits' College, with the ceremonies of the R. C. Church.

† Three Nuns of the Hôtel-Dieu Convent, according to authorities quoted by Mr. Faucher, were buried in the vault (*caveau*) of the Jesuits' Chapel. The sisterhood had been allowed the use of a wing of the Jesuits' College, where they removed after the conflagration of the 7th June, 1755, which destroyed their hospital.

4° Mère Marie Marthe Desroches de Saint-François-Xavier, a young woman of 28 years, who succumbed to small pox on the 16th August, 1755.

5° Mère de l Enfant-Jésus, who expired on the 12th May, 1756.

6° Mère de Sainte-Monique, who died in July, 1756, the victim of her devotion in ministering to the decimated crew of the *ship Léopard* sunk in the port by order of Government to arrest the spread of the pestilential disease which had raged on the passage out. Mr. Faucher closes his able report with a suggestion that a monument ought to be raised, to commemorate the labors and devotion of the Jesuits, on the denuded area on which stood their venerable College.

*Relation de ce qui s'est passé lors des Fouilles faites par ordre du Gouvernement dans une partie des fondations du COLLÉGE DES JÉSUITES de Québec, précédée de certaines observations par FAUCHER DE SAINT MAURICE. Québec. C. Darveau—1879.*

under lock and key in a wooden box; and in September, 1878, the whole was placed in a small but substantial stone structure, in the court of the Jesuit Barracks, known as the "Regimental Magazine," pending their delivery for permanent disposal to Rev. Père Sachez, Superior of the Jesuits Order in Quebec.

In May, 1879, on opening this magazine, it was found that the venerable bones, box and all had disappeared, the staple of the padlock on the door having been forced. By whom and for what purpose, the robbery?

Let us walk on, and view with the Professor's eyes the adjoining public edifice, which stood here in 1749, the Récollet Convent "a spacious building," says Kalm, "two story high, with a large orchard and kitchen garden."

Its Church or Chapel was, on 6th September, 1796, destroyed by fire; two eye-witnesses of the conflagration, Philippe Aubert DeGaspé and Deputy-Commissary-General James Thompson, the first in his *Memoires*, the second in his unpublished *Diary*, have vividly portrayed the accident. The Church faced the Ring and the old Château; it formed part of the Récollet Convent, "a vast quadrangular building, with a court and well stocked orchard" on Garden street; it was occasionally used as a state prison. The Huguenot and agitater, Pierre DuCalvet, spent some dreary days in its cells in 1781-84; and during the summer of 1776, a young volunteer under Benedict Arnold, John Joseph Henry, (who lived to become a distinguished Pennsylvania Judge) was immured in this monastery, after his arrest by the British, at the unsuccessful attack in the Lower Town, in Sault-au-Matelot street, on 31st December, 1775, as he graphically relates in his *Memoirs*. It was a monastery of the order of Saint Francis. The Provincial, in 1793, a well known, witty, jovial and eccentric personage, Father Félix DeBerrey, had more than once dined and wined His Royal Highness, Prince Edward, the father of our Gracious Sovereign, when stationed in our garrison in 1791-4, with his regiment the 7th Fusileers.

The Récollet Church was also a sacred and last resting place for the illustrious dead. Of the six French Governors who expired at Quebec, four slept within its silent vaults, until the translation, in 1796, of their ashes to the vaults of the Basilica, viz : (1) Frontenac, (2) de Callières, (3) Vaudreuil, (4) de la Jonquière. Governor deMesy had been buried in the Hôtel-Dieu Chapel, and the first Governor, de Champlain, 'tis generally believed, was interred near the Château Saint Louis, in a "sépulchre particulier," near the spot now surmounted by his bust, beneath the soil, on which, in 1871, was erected the new Post Office.

On the south-west side of the Château, could be seen a building devoted to the administration of Justice, La Senechaussée,† (Séneschal's Jurisdiction,) and which bore the name of " The Palace." It was doubtless there that, in 1664, the Supreme Council held its sessions. In 1665 it was assigned to the Marquis de Tracy, for a residence whilst in the colony. From the *Place D'Armes*, the higher road (*Grande Allée*) took its departure and led to Cap Rouge. On the right and left of this road, were several small lots of land given to certain persons for the purpose of being built upon. The Indian Fort was that entrenchment of

---

The following inscription was on the coffin plate :

(1) Count Frontenac—"Cy gyt le Haut et Puissant Seigneur, Louis de Buade, Comte de Frontenac, Gouverneur-Général de la Nouvelle-France. Mort à Québec, le 28 novembre 1698."—(*Hist. of Canada, Smith, Vol. I. P. 153.*)

(2) Gov. deCallières.—"Cy gyst Haut et Puissant Seigneur, Hector deCallières, Chevalier de Saint-Louis, Gouverneur et Lieutenant-Général de la Nouvello-France, décédé le 26 mai 1703."—(*Ibid., P. 148.*)

(3) Gov. de Vaudreuil.—"Cy gist Haut et Puissant Seigneur, Messire Philippe Rigaud, Marquis de Vaudreuil, Grande Croix de l'Ordre Militaire de Saint-Louis, Gouverneur et Lieutenant-Général de toute la Nouvelle-France, décédé le dixième octobre 1725."—(*Ibid., P. 190.*)

(4) M. de la Jonquière.—"Cy repose le corps de Messire Jacques-Pierre de Taffanell, Marquis de la Jonquière, Baron de Castelnau, Seigneur de Hardarsmagnas et autres lieux, Commandeur de l'Ordre Royal et Militaire de Saint-Louis, Chef d'Escadre des Armées Navales, Gouverneur et Lieutenant-Général pour le Roy en toute la Nouvelle-France, terres et passes de la Louisiano. Décédé à Québec, lo 17 mai 1752, à six heures-et-demie du soir, âgé de 67 ans."—(*Ibid., P. 222.*)

† It appears to have stood at the east end of St. Louis street—where the residence and office of Jas. Dunbar, Esq., Q.C., now stands.

which we have spoken, which served as a last hiding place
to the sad remains of the once powerful Huron nation,
forming in all eighty-four souls, in the year 1665. It continued to be occupied by them up to the peace with the
Iroquois. After the arrival of the troops, they took their
departure in order to devote themselves to the cultivation
of the lands.

Besides the buildings of the Reverend Jesuit Fathers,
those of the Ursulines (nuns,) and those of the Hospital
(Hôtel-Dieu,) in the Upper Town, could be seen a house
situated behind the Altar part of the Parish Church, where
dwelt Monseigneur de Laval. It was, probably, what he
called his Seminary, and where he caused some young men
to be educated, destined afterwards for the priesthood.

It was at the Seminary, the worthy Prelate resided with
his priests, to the number of eight which, at that period,
comprised all the secular clergy of Quebec. There, also,
was the Church of Notre-Dame in the form of a Latin
cross.*

Couillard Street calls up one of the most important
personages of the era of Champlain, Guillaume Couillard,
the ancester of Madame Alexandre deLéry *née* Couillard.
It would fill a volume to retrace the historical incidents
which attach themselves to "La Grande Place du Fort" (now
called the *Ring*.) We have pointed out a goodly number
in the first pages (10-16,) of the " Album du Touriste." To
what we have already said we shall add the following
details :

It would appear that on the site upon which the Union
Hall was built,‖ (1805,) now occupied by the offices of the
*Journal de Québec, &c.*, resided the Governor D'Aillebout,

---

* Faillon, Vol. III, p. 372.

‖ The laying of the corner stone of this lofty building whose proportions
must have seemed colossal to our fathers, was done with grand masonic
honors on the 14th August, 1805, by the Hon. Thos. Dunn, President of the

about the year 1650.  He had reserved to himself, on the 10th
January, 1649, the strip of ground comprised between
Fort and Treasury streets on the one side, and the streets
Buade and Ste. Anne on the other side.  At the corner of
Treasury and Buade streets, on the west, Jean Côté possessed
a piece of ground (*emplacement*) which he presented as a
dowery in 1649, to his daughter Simonne who married
Pierre Soumandre.

The grounds of the Archbishop's Palace formed part of
the field possessed by Couillard, whose house stood in the
now existing garden of the Seminary, opposite the gate
which faces the principal alley, the foundations of which
were discovered and brought to light by the Abbé Laverdière, in 1866.

---

Province of Lower Canada, and administrator of the Government, assisted
by William Holmes, Esq., M.D., Deputy Grand Master of Ancient and Accepted
Free Masons.  Several coins of that reign were deposited under the stone.
Amongst the members of the craft, we find the names of Joseph Bouchette,
Claude Dénéchaud, Joseph Plante, Angus Shaw, Thomas Place, David Monro ;
the architect's name is Edward Cannon, grand-father of Messrs. Ed. J., Lawrence and James Cannon, our esteemed fellow citizens ;  Rev. Dr. Spark
delivered a splendid oration, to be found in the *Quebec Mercury*, of 17th
August, 1805.

Hujusce Fori Municipalis, Anglicè UNION HALL, ex Senatus provincialis
consulto erecti.
THOMAS DUNN Vir Honorabilis Provinciæ Prefectus Politiæque Adminis-
trator,
Adstantibus et Curatoribus Selectis.
Hon. *John Young* Præse, Hon. *John Antoine Panet* Comitiæ Provincialis
Rogatore,
*Jonathan Sewell* Armigero Cognitore Regio,
*John Painter* et *John Blackwood*, Armigeris, Pacis Curatoribus ;
*Joseph Bouchette* Armigero Mensorum Principali,
*John Caldwell, Claude Dénéchaud, John Coltman, John Taylor, Joseph
Plante, Angus Shaw, Thomas Place* et *David Monro*, de Quebec Armigeris,
Nec non et multis *Latomorum* hujus Urbis, quorum *William Holmes* Armiger
M D fuit summus Magister Deputatus, adjuvantibus, hunc primum Lapidem
posuit, dei XIV.  Mensis Sextilis, Anno Salutis MDCCCV.
Nummi quoque Regis Regnantis
GEORGII III.
Suppositi sunt,
*Videlicet.*
Nummus Aureus Anglicè *Guinea*, aureum etiam Dimidium ejus et Triens;
Nummus argenteus solidos quinque Anglicos valans, solidus dimidium solidi,
et quarta pars; nummus Æranus denarios duos Anglicos valens; denariu-
obolus; et quadrans.
EDWARD CANNON,
Architectus.

6

On the conspicuous site where stands the unpretending brick structure known as our present House of Parliament, (which succeeded the handsone cut stone edifice burnt, in 1854,) one might, in 1660, have seen the dwelling of a man of note, Ruette d'Auteuil. D'Auteuil became subsequently Attorney General and had lively times with that sturdy old ruler, Count de Frontenac. Ruette d'Auteuil had sold the lot for $600 (3,000 livres de 20 sols) to Major Provost, who resold it with the two story stone house thereon erected, for $3,000, to Bishop St. Vallier. The latter having bequeathed it to his ecclesiastical successor, Bishop Plessis ceded it to the Imperial Government for an annual ground rent of £1,000 —this rent is continued to the Archbishop by the Provincial Government of Quebec : no one now cares to enquire why Bishop Plessis made such an excellent bargain, though a cause is assigned.

Palace Street was thus denominated from its leading direct from the Upper Town to the Intendant's Palace —latterly the King's woodyard.* In earlier days it went by the name of *Rue des Pauvres*, (Street of the Poor,) from its intersecting the domain of the *Hôtel Dieu*, whose revenues were devoted to the maintenance of the poor, sheltered behind its massive old walls. Close by, on Saint John street, Bishop St. Vallier had founded *le Bureau des Pauvres*, where the beggars of Quebec (a thriving class to this day) received alms, in order to deter them from begging in the country round the city. The success which crowned this humble retreat of the mendicant led the philantrophic bishop to found the General Hospital at St. Roch.

At the western corner of Palace and St. John streets, has stood since 1771, a well known land mark : a wooden statue of General Wolfe, sculptured by the Brothers Cholette,

---

* On a portion of it, a cattle market has been built—under French rule, it formed a beautiful park for the magnificent Intendants.

at the request of George Hipps, a loyal butcher. The peregrinations of this historic relic, in 1838, from Quebec to Halifax—from Halifax to Bermuda, hence to Portsmouth, and finally to its old niche at Wolfe's corner St. John Street, whilst they afforded much sport to the middies of H. M. Ship *Inconstant*, who visited our port that summer and carried away the General, were the subject of several newspaper paragraphs in prose and in verse.

Finally, the safe return of the "General" with a bran new coat of paint and varnish in a deal box, consigned to His Worship, the Mayor (Thomas Pope) of Quebec, sent by unknown hands, was made an occasion for rejoicing to every friend of the British hero, whom Quebec contained and they were not few.

Some of the actors of this practical joke, staunch upholders of Britannia's sovereignty of the sea, now pace their quarter deck, t'is said, proud and stern admirals!

The street and hill leading down from the parochial Church, (whose title was *Cathedral of the Immaculate Conception of the Blessed Virgin Mary*,) to the outlet, where Hope Gate was built in 1786, was called Ste. Famille street—from its vicinity to the Cathedral. On the east side, half way up the hill still exists the old homestead of the deLéry—in 1854, occupied by Sir E. P. Taché, since, sold to the Quebec Seminary. On the opposite side a little higher up, also survives the old house of M. Jean Langevin, father of the Bishop of Rimouski, Hon. H. L. Langevin and others. Here in the closing days of French Dominion lived the first Acadian, who brought to Quebec the news of the dispersion of his compatriots, so eloquently sung by Longfellow : Dr. Lajus, of French extraction, who settled at Quebec, and married a sister of Bishop Hubert ; on the northern angle of this old tenement you now read " *Ste. Famille* street."

That dear old street,—St. George street, formerly,—now called after the first inhabitant of the Upper Town in 1617, *Louis Hébert*, by the erection of the lofty Medical College and Laval University, for us has been shorn of its name—its sunshine—its glory, since the home * of our youth, at the east end, has passed in foreign hands. It is now *Hébert* street.

Laval, Attorney-General D'Auteuil, Louis de Buade, *Ste-Hélène*, (†) seem to come back to life in the ancient streets of the same name, whilst Frontenac, Iberville, Fiedmont, are brought to one's recollection, in the modern thoroughfares. The old Scotch pilot, Abraham Martin, (who, according to the Jesuits' Journal, was a bit of a scamp, though he does not appear to have been tried for his peccadiloes,) owned a domain of thirty-two acres of land in St. John's suburbs, which were bounded, towards the north, by the hill which now bears his name (*La Côte d'Abraham*.)

Mythology has exacted a tribute on a strip of ground in the St. Louis suburbs. The chief priest of the pagan Olympus boasts of his lane, "Jupiter street" called after a celebrated inn, Jupiter's Inn, on account of a full sized statue of the master of Olympus which stood formerly over the main entrance. In the beginning of the century, a mineral spring of wondrous efficacy attracted to this neighborhood, those of our *fashionables* whose liver was out of order; alas! like that of some other famous springs, its efficacy is a thing of the past!

Modern astronomy is represented in Arago street. ‡

* The old homestead successively owned by Messrs. Timothy H. Dunn and Joseph Shehyn, M.P.P., was erected for Capt. Benjamin LeMoine, Canad. Volt., the writer's father, in 1812.

† LeMoine de Ste Hélène. It is also asserted this street (Ste. Hélène,) was named after the Reverend Mother Ste. Hélène, Superioress of the Hôtel-Dieu—(Dlle Regnard du Plessis).

‡ We read in the Municipal Registrar, "Alfred street extends from Colombe street to Arago street, in the Fief Notre-Dame des Anges. This street as well as those which run parallel with it, Alexandre, Nelson, Turgeon, Jérôme and St. Ours, and the transecting streets, Arago and Colombe, were laid out in 1845, thirty feet in width (St. Ours street, only having forty feet in width,) by the Inspector of Roads, M. Joseph Hamel, pursuant to the instructions, and with the consent of the Religious Ladies (nuns) of the General Hospital."

Parloir street leads to the *parloir*† of the Ursulines. Here resided the late Judge de Bonne, at the dawn of the present century ; the Ursulines have named, after their patron Saint, Ste. Ursule, the first street to the west, which intersects at right angles, St. Louis and Ste. Anne streets. Ste. Ursule and Ste. Anne streets and environs, seem to have been specially appropriated by the disciples of Hippocrates. Physicians and Surgeons there assuredly do congregate, viz. : Dr. James Sewell, his son, Dr. Collin Sewell, Drs. Landry, Lemieux, Boswell, Belleau, Russell, Russell, jr., Gale, Ross, Baillargeon, Roy, Fortier, LaRue, Parke, Rowand, Henchey, Vallée, Marsden, Jackson, distinguished physicians all. Notwithstanding that it is the abode of so many eminent members of the Faculty, the locality is healthy ; nay, conducive to longevity.

The streets Craig, Carleton, Haldimand, Dalhousie, Hope, Richmond, Prevost, Aylmer, perpetuate the memory of eight English Governors. Many of the luxurious dwellings on the Cape date back to 1810 or so ; this now aristocratic neighborhood, after the conquest and until 1830, was occupied by carters, old French market gardeners and descendants of French artisans, &c ,—such were the early tenants of *Des Carrières, Mont Carmel, Ste. Geneviève, St. Denis, Des Grisons* streets.—*Mais nous avons changé tout cela.*

A few years since, the Town Council, on motion of Councillor Ernest Gagnon, whose name is identified with our popular songs,§ disturbed the nomenclature of that part of D'Aiguillon Street, *extra muros*, by substituting the name of " Charlevoix." To that section of St. Joseph street, *intra muros*, was conferred the name of our respected historian, F. X. Garneau. To St. François street, the name of the historian, Ferland, was awarded ; the historian, Rob. Christie, has also his street ; this met with general approval.

† The *Parloir* is the name of the room in which the young ladies speak to their relatives and friends visiting them.

§ *Chansons populaires du Canada*, &c., par Ernest Gagnon, 1865.

Our thoroughfares, our promenades, even in those dreary months, when the northern blast howls over the Canadian landscape, have some blithsome gleams of sunshine. Never shall we forget one bright, frosty January afternoon, about four o'clock, in the year 1872, when solitary, though not sad, standing on Durham Terrace, was unveiled to us "a most magnificent picture, a scene of glorified nature painted by the hand of the Creator. The setting sun had charged the skies with all its gorgeous heraldry of purple and crimson and gold, and the tints were diffused and reflected through fleecy clouds, becoming softer and richer through expansion. The mountain tops, wood-crowned, where the light and shadow appeared to be struggling for mastery, stood out in relief from the white plain, and stretching away in indistinct, dreamy distances finally seemed to blend with the painted skies. The ice-covered bay was lit up with glowing shades, in contrast with the deep blue of the clear water beyond; from which the island rose, and into which the point jutted with grand picturesqueness; the light played through the frost glistening, but still sombre pines, and spreading out over deserted fields. Levis and the South Shore received not so much of the illumination, and the grimness of the citadel served as a contrast and a relief to the eye bewildered with the unaccustomed grandeur. But as the sun sank deeper behind the eternal hills, shadows began to fall, and the bright colors toned down to the grey of dusk; stars shone out, the gray was chased away, and the azure. diamond dotted skies told not of the glory of sunset which had so shortly before suffused them."—(*Morning Chronicle*.)

We have just seen described the incomparable panorama which a winter sunset disclosed from the lofty promenade, to which the Earl of Dufferin* has bequeathed

---

* One of the boons conferred through the gifted nobleman on Quebec, and we take pleasure in proclaiming it, is the superb, world-renowned Terrace, now bearing his name, "Dufferin Terrace."

his name. Let us now accompany one of our genial summer
butterflies, fluttering through the mazes of old Stadacona
escorting a bride ; let us listen to H. W. D. Howells in the
WEDDING JOURNEY. "Nothing, I think, more enforces
the illusion of Southern Europe in Quebec than the
Sunday-night promenading on the Durham (now Dufferin)
Terrace. This is the ample span on the brow of the cliff
to the left of the citadel, the noblest and most commanding
position in the whole city, which was formerly occupied by
the old Castle of St. Louis, where dwelt the brave Count
Frontenac and his splendid successors of the French
regime. The castle went the way of Quebec by fire some
forty years ago, (23rd January, 1834), and Lord Durham levelled the site and made it a public promenade. A stately arcade
of solid masonry supports it on the brink of the rock, and
an iron parapet incloses it ; there are a few seats to lounge
upon, and some idle old guns for the children to clamber
over and play with. A soft twilight had followed the day,
and there was just enough obscurity to hide from a willing
eye the Northern and New World facts of the scene, and
to leaving into more romantic relief the citadel dark against
the mellow evening, and the people gossiping from window
to window across the narrow streets of the Lower Town.
The Terrace itself was densely thronged, and there was a
constant coming and going of the promenaders, and each
formally paced back and forth upon the planking for a
certain time, and then went quietly home giving place to
new arrivals. They were nearly all French, and they were
not generally, it seemed, of the first fashion, but rather of
middling condition in life ; the English being represented
only by a few young fellows, and now and then a red
faced old gentleman with an Indian scarf trailing from his
hat. There were some fair American costumes and faces
in the crowd, but it was essentially Quebecian. The
young girls walked in pairs, or with their lovers, had the
true touch of provincial unstylishness, the young men the

inellectual excess of the second-rate Latin dandy, the elder the rude inelegance of a *bourgeoisie* in them; but a few better-figured *avocats* or *notaires* (their profession was as unmistakable as if they had carried their well-polished doorplates upon their breasts), walked and gravely talked with each other. The non-American character of the scene was not less vividly marked in the fact, that each person dressed according to his own taste and frankly indulged private shapes and colours. One of the promenaders was in white, even to his canvas shoes; another, with yet bolder individuality, appeared in perfect purple. It had a strange, almost portentous effect when these two startling figures met as friends and joined with each other in the promenade with united arms; but the evening was nearly beginning to darken round them, and presently the purple comrade was merely a sombre shadow beside the glimmering white.

The valleys and the heights now vanished; but the river defined itself by the varicolored light of the ships and steamers that lay, dark motionless hulks upon its broad breast; the lights of Point Levis swarmed upon the other shore; the Lower Town, two hundred feet below them, stretched an alluring mystery of clustering roofs and lamp-lit windows, and dark and shining streets around the mighty rock, mural-crowned. Suddenly a spectacle peculiarly Northern and characteristic of Quebec revealed itself; a long arch brightened over the northern horizon; the tremulous flames of the aurora, pallid violet or faintly tinged with crimson, shot upward from it, and played with a vivid apparition and evanescence to the zenith. While the stranger looked, a gun boomed from the citadel, and the wild sweet notes of the bugle sprang out upon the silence."

## CHAP. II.

Prince Edward street, St. Roch, and "Donnacona" street, near the Ursulines, bring up the memory of two important personages of the past, Edward Augustus, Duke of Kent—an English Prince, and Donnacona, a swarthy chief of primitive Canada.

The vanquisher of Montcalm, General Wolfe, is honored not only by a statue, at the corner of Palace and St. John's streets, (1) but again by the street which bears his name, Wolfe street. In like manner, his illustrious rival Montcalm, claims an entire section of the city "Montcalm Ward." Can it be that the susceptible young Captain of the "Albemarle," Horatio Nelson, carried on his flirtation with the captivating Miss Mary Simpson, in 1782, in the street which now rejoices in his name? Several streets in the St. Louis, St. John, and St. Roch suburbs, bear the names of eminent citizens who have, at different periods, made a free gift of the sites or, who, by their public spirit, have left behind them a cherished memory among the people : Messrs. Berthelot, D'Artigny, Grey Stewart, T. C. Lee, Buteau, Hudon, Smith, Salaberry, Scott, Tourangeau, Pozer, Panet, Bell, Robitaille, Ryland, St. Ours.

The width of the greater number of the streets of the city vary from thirty to forty feet; the broadest is Crown street. Well do the proprietors deserve our congratulations for the beautiful shade trees which they have caused to be there planted.

Quebec comprises about ten small *Fiefs* or Domaines. The *Fief* Sault-au-Matelot (the sailor's leap) belongs to the Seminary. The Ursulines, the Church (*Fabrique*), the

(1) St. John street is thirty-six feet in width, *intra muros*, and forty-six in width, *extra muros*, in consequence of a gift of ten feet of ground, by the proprietors, after the great fire of 1845.

7

Heirs LaRue, the Hôtel-Dieu, the *Récollets* Friars, each had its Fief. The Church possesses a domaine besides that of Cape Diamond. The *Fief "de la Miséricorde,"* (Mercy), belongs to the Hôtel-Dieu. The Heirs LaRue possess the *Fief de Bécancour*, and that of *De Villeraie*; there is also the *Fief Sasseville*. The *"Fief of the Récollets"* now belongs to the Crown.

St. Roch owes a debt of gratitude to Monseigneur de Saint-Valier, whose name is identified with the street which he so often perambulated in his visits to the General Hospital, where he terminated his useful career. His Lordship seems to have entertained a particular attachment for the locality where he had founded this hospital, where he resided, in order to rent his Mountain Hill Palace to Intendant Talon, and thus save the expense of a Chaplain. The General Hospital was the third Asylum for the infirm, which the Bishop had founded. Subsequently, came the Intendant de Meulles who, towards 1684, endowed the eastern portion of the quarter with an edifice (the Intendant's Palace) remarkable for its dimensions, its magnificence and its ornate gardens.

Where Talon (a former Intendant) had left a brewery in a state of ruin and about seventeen acres of land unoccupied, Louis XIV., by the advice of his Intendant de Meulles, lavished vast sums of money in the erection of a sumptuous palace in which French justice was administered and in which, at a later period, under Bigot, it was *purchasable.* Our illustrious ancestors, for that matter, were not the kind of men to weep over such trifles, imbued as they were from infancy with the feudal system and all its irksome duties, without forgetting the forced labour (*corvées*) and those admirable "Royal Secret-warrants," (*lettres de cachet*). What did the institutions of a free people, the text of *Magna Charta* signify to them?

On this spot stood the notorious warehouse, where Bigot, Cadet and their confederates retailed, at enormous profits, the provisions and supplies which King Louis XV. doled out in 1758, to the starving inhabitants of Quebec. The people christened the house "*La Friponne*," (*The Knavery!!*) Near the site of Talon's old brewery (which had been converted into a prison in 1634, by *Frontenac*, and which held fast until his trial the *Abbé de Fénélon*, (2) now stands the "Anchor Brewery." (Boswell's.)

Doubtless to the eyes of the "Free and Independent Electors" of La Vacherie in 1759, the Intendant's Palace seemed a species of "Eighth Wonder.' The Eighth Wonder lost much of its *éclat*, however, by the inauguration of English rule, in 1759, but a total eclipse came over this imposing and majestic luminary, when Guy Carleton's guns from the ramparts of Quebec, began, in 1775, to thunder on its cupola and roof, which offered a shelter to Arnold's soldiery : the rabble of "shoe-makers, hatters, blacksmiths and inn-keepers," (says Colonel Henry Caldwell), bent on providing Canada with the blessings of republicanism. We have just mentioned "*La Vacherie*," this consisted of the extensive and moist pastures at the foot of *Coteau Sainte-Geneviève*, towards the General Hospital where the city cows were grazed ; on this site and gracing the handsome streets "Crown," "Craig" and "Desfossés," can now be seen elegant dry-goods stores vying with the largest in the Upper Town. Had St. Peter street, in 1775, been provided with a regular way of communication with St. Roch ; had St. Paul street then existed, the sun of progress would have shone there nearly a century earlier.

(2) The *Abbé de Fénélon* was the half brother of the illustrious Archbishop of *Cambrai*, the author of "Telemachus." He was tried by *Frontenac* and the Supreme Council for having, at the preceding Easter, preached a violent sermon against the *corvées* (enforced labour) to build up *Fort Frontenac*, &c. He refused to acknowledge the competency of the tribunal to try him, appeared before it with his hat on, &c. *Frontenac* had him committed for contempt. Altogether, it was a curious squabble, the decision of which was ultimately left to the French King.

" For a considerable time past, several plans of ameliora-
tion of the City of Quebec," says the Abbé Ferland, " were
proposed to the ministry by *M. de Meulles*. The absolute
necessity of obtaining a desirable locality for the residence
of the *Intendant*, and for the holding of the sessions of the
Council, the *Château Saint Louis* being hardly sufficient to
afford suitable quarters for the Governor and the persons
who formed his household. M. de Meulles proposed
purchasing, a large stone building which M. Talon had
caused to be erected for the purpose of a brewery and
which, for several years, had remained unoccupied. Placed
in a very commodious position on the bank of the river St.
Charles, and not many steps from the Upper Town, this
edifice with suitable repairs and additions, might furnish
not alone a desirable residence for the *Intendant*, but also,
halls and offices for the Supreme Council and the Courts
of Justice, as likewise, vaults for the archives, and a prison
for the criminals." Adjacent to the old Brewery, M. Talon
owned an extent of land of about seventeen superficial
acres of which no use was made in M. de Meulles' plan; a
certain portion of this land could be reserved for the
gardens and dependencies of the Intendant's Palace, whilst
the remainder might be portioned off into building lots
(*emplacements*) and thus convert it into a second lower town
and which might some day, be extended to the foot of the
Cape. He believed that if this plan were adopted the new
buildings of Quebec would extend in that direction and not
on the heights almost exclusively occupied by the Religious
Communities."(1)

## CHAP. III.

We perceive, according to Mr. Panet's Journal, that Saint
Roch existed in 1759; that the women and children,
residents of that quarter, were not wholly indifferent to
the fate of their distressed country, " the same day, (31st

---

(1) *Cours d'Histoire du Canada*, Vol. 2, p. 140.

July, 1759)," says Panet, "we heard a great uproar in the St. Roch quarter, the women and children were shouting, 'Long live the King!,'" (2) "I ascended the height (on the *Coteau Ste. Geneviève*) and there beheld the first frigate all in a blaze, very shortly afterwards, a black smoke issuing from the second which blew up and afterwards took on fire." On the 4th August, several bomb-shells of 80, fell on Saint Roch. We read, that on the 31st August, two soldiers were hanged at three o'clock in the afternoon for having stolen a cask of brandy from the house of one Charland, in the Saint Roch quarter. In those times the General (or *the Recorder*,) did not do things by halves. Who was this Charland of 1759? Could he be the same who, sixteen years afterwards, fought so stoutly together with Dambourgès at the Sault-au-Matelot engagement? Since the inauguration of the English domination, Saint Roch became peopled in a most rapid manner; we now see there a net-work of streets embracing in extent several leagues.

The most ancient highway of the quarter (St. Roch,) is probably St. Valier street. "Desfossés" street most likely derives its name from the ditches (*fossés*) which served to drain the green pastures of *La Vacherie*. The old Bridge street dates from the end of the last century (1789). "Dorchester" street recalls the esteemed and popular administrator Lord Dorchester, who, under the name of Guy Carleton, led on to victory the militia of Quebec in 1775.

"Craig" street received its name from Sir James Craig, a gouty, testy, but trusted old soldier, who administered the Government in 1807 ; it was enlarged and widened ten feet, after the great fire of 1845. The site of St. Paul's Market was acquired from the Royal Ordinance, on 31st July, 1831.

---

(2) Louis XV.

"Dorchester" Bridge was constructed in 1822, and took the place of the former bridge (Vieux Pont) on the street to the west, built by Asa Porter in 1789, and called after Lord Dorchester, the "Saviour of Quebec." Saint Joseph street, St. Roch, which, at one period, had a width of only twenty-five feet, was widened to the extent of forty, through the liberality of certain persons. From this circumstance, the corporation was induced to continue it beyond the city limits up to the road which leads to Lorette, thereby rendering it the most useful and one of the handsomest streets of Saint Roch.

At what period did the most spacious highway of the ward, ("Crown" street, sixty feet in width), receive its baptismal name? Most assuredly, it was previous to 1837, the democratic era of Papineau. "King" street, no doubt, recalls the reign of George III. So also does "Queen" street, recall his Consort.

Towards the year 1815, the late Honorable John Richardson, of Montreal, conferred his name on the street which intersects the grounds which the Crown had then conceded to him, for the heirs of the late William Grant, late Receiver General who, likewise, bequeathed his name to a street adjacent. A Mr. Henderson (1) about the commencement of the present century, possessed grounds in the vicinity of the present Gas works, hence we have "Henderson" street. The Gas Company's Wharf is built on the site of the old jetty of which we have seen mention made, about 1720. This long pier was composed of large boulders heaped one upon the other, and served the purpose of sheltering the landing place at the *Palais* harbour, from the northeast winds. In 1815, Colonel Bouchette, says it was a promenade pretty well frequented.

---

(1) This gentleman (Mr. William Henderson), was for many years Secretary of the Quebec Fire Assurance Company. I believe he is still living and that he resides at Frampton, in the County of Dorchester, P. Q. (C. A.)

In the present day, the prolongation of the wharf has left no trace of it; the Station of the North Shore Railway covers a portion of this area.

"Church" street (la rue de l'Eglise), doubtless owes its name to the erection of the beautiful Saint Roch Church, towards 1812, the site of which was given by the late Honorable John Mure, who died in Scotland in 1823.

Saint Roch, like the Upper Town, comprises several *Fiefs*, proceeding from the *Fief* of the Seminary and reaching as far as the Gas wharf; the beaches with the right of fishing, belonged originally to the *Hôtel-Dieu* by a concession dated the 21st March, 1648, but they have been conceded to others. The Crown possesses an important reserve towards the west of this grant; then comes the grant made, in 1814 or 1815, to the heirs William Grant, now occupied by several ship-yards. Jacques Cartier, who, in 1535-6, wintered in the vicinity of Saint Roch, left his name to an entire municipal division of this rich suburb as well as to a spacious market hall. (The Jacques Cartier Market Hall.)

## CHAP. IV.

Let us descend that ancient and tortuous Lower Town Hill which has re-echoed the tread of so many regiments, in which so many Governors, French and English have, on divers occasions, heard themselves enthusiastically cheered by admiring crowds, the hill which viceroys of France and of England, from the ostentatious Marquis de Tracy to the proud Earl of Durham, ascended on their way to the *Chateau* Saint Louis, surrounded by their brilliant staff and saluted by cannon and with warlike flourish of trumpets!

In earlier times, the military and religious display was blended with an aroma of literature and elaborate Indian oratory, combining prose and poetry.

Francis Parkman will tell us of what took place on the arrival, on the 28th July, 1658, of the Viscount D'Argenson, the Governor of the colony :—" When Argenson arrived to assume the government, a curious greeting had awaited him. The Jesuits asked him to dine ; vespers followed the repast ; and then they conducted him into a hall where the boys of their school—disguised, one as the Genius of New France, one as the Genius of the Forest, and others as Indians of various friendly tribes—made him speeches by turn, in prose and in verse. First, Pierre du Quet, who played the Genius of New France, presented his Indian retinue to the Governor, in a complimentary harangue. Then four other boys, personating French colonists, made him four flattering addresses, in French verse. Charles Denis, dressed as a Huron, followed, bewailing the ruin of his people, and appealing to Argenson for aid. Jean François Bourdon, in the character of an Algonquin, next advanced on the platform, boasted his courage, and declared that he was ashamed to cry like the Huron. The Genius of the Forest now appeared, with a retinue of wild Indians from the interior, who being unable to speak French, addressed the Governor in their native tongues, which the Genius proceeded to interpret. Two other boys in the character of prisoners just escaped from the Iroquois, then came forward imploring aid in piteous accents; and in conclusion the whole troop of Indians from far and near laid their bows and arrows at the feet of Argenson, and hailed him as their chief.

Besides these mock Indians, a crowd of genuine savages had gathered at Quebec to greet the new "Onouthio." On the next day—at his own cost, as he writes to a friend—he gave them a feast, consisting of seven large kettlesful of Indian corn, peas, prunes, sturgeon, eels and fat, which they devoured, he says, after having first sung me a song, after their fashion."

Probably one of the most gorgeous displays on record, was that attending the arrival of the great Marquis of Tracy, in 1665. He came with a brilliant staff, a crowd of young nobles; and accompanied by two hundred soldiers, to be followed by a thousand more of the dashing regiment of Carignan-Salières. "He sailed up the St. Lawrence, and on the thirtieth of June, 1665, anchored in the basin of Quebec. The broad, white standard, blazoned with the arms of France, proclaimed the representative of royalty; and Point Levi and Cape Diamond and the distant Cape Tourmente roared back the sound of the saluting cannon. All Quebec was on the ramparts or at the landing place, and all eyes were strained at the two vessels as they slowly emptied their crowded decks into the boats alongside. The boats at length drew near, and the lieutenant-general and his suite landed on the quay with a pomp such as Quebec had never seen before.

Tracy was a veteran of sixty-two, portly and tall, "one of the largest men I ever saw," writes Mother Mary; but he was sallow with disease, for fever had seized him, and it had fared ill with him on the long voyage. The Chevalier de Chaumont walked at his side, and young nobles surrounded him, gorgeous in lace and ribbons, and majestic in leonine wigs. Twenty-four guards in the King's livery led the way, followed by four pages and six valets* ; and thus, while the Frenchmen shouted and the Indians stared, the august procession threaded the streets of the Lower Town, and climbed the steep pathway that scaled the cliffs above. Breathing hard, they reached the top, passed on the left the dilapidated walls of the fort and the shed of mingled wood and masonry which then bore the name of the Castle of St. Louis; passed on the right the old house of Couillard and the site of Laval's new seminary, and soon reached the square betwixt the Jesuit college and the Cathedral.

---

* "His constant attendance when he went abroad," says Mère Juchereau.

The bells were ringing in a phrensy of welcome. Laval in pontificals, surrounded by priests and Jesuits, stood waiting to receive the deputy of the King, and as he greeted Tracy and offered him the holy water, he looked with anxious curiosity to see what manner of man he was. The signs were auspicious. The deportment of the lieutenant-general left nothing to desire. A *prie-dieu* had been placed for him. He declined it. They offered him a cushion, but he would not have it, and fevered as he was, he knelt on the bare pavement with a devotion that edified every beholder. *Te Deum* was sung and a day of rejoicing followed." §

In our day, we can recall but one pageant at all equal: the roar of cannon, &c., attending the advent of the great Earl of Durham, but there were noticeable fewer "priests," fewer "Jesuits," and less "kneeling" in the procession.

Line-of-battle ships—stately frigates, twelve in number: the *Malabar—Hastings—Cornwallis—Inconstant—Hercules—Pique—Charybdis—Pearl—Vestal—Medea—Dee—* and *Andromache* escorted to our shores, the able, proud, humane,† but unlucky Vice-Roy and High Commissioner, with his clever advisers—the Turtons, Bullers, Wakefields, Hansomes, Derbyshires, Dunkins, *cum multis aliis*.

Here we stand on the principal artery of the commerce of the ancient city, Saint Peter street, having a width of only twenty-four feet. St. Peter street is probably more ancient than its sister *Sault-au-Matelot* street.

On the site on which the "Quebec Bank" (2) was erected in 1863, there stood the offices, the vaults, and the wharf

---

§ The *Old Régime in Canada.* p. 177-9.

† I use the term advisedly, for had he followed out the Colborne policy and gibetted the "Bermuda exiles," he would have had one sin less to atone for, at the hands of Lord Brougham and other merciless enemies in England.

(2) Thanks to the late Mr. J. B. Martel, then Secretary of the Harbour Commission, Quebec, we may designate in a few words the site which the Quebec Bank now possesses. This extent of ground (at that period a beach lot), was conceded to the Seminary by the *Marquis de Denonville* in 1687, and confirm-

of the well-known merchant, John Lymburner. There were three Lymburners : John, lost at sea in the fall of 1775, Matthew, and Adam the most able of the three ; they were, no doubt, related to each other. The loyalty of Adam, towards the British Crown, in 1775, was more than suspected ; his oratorical powers, however, and his knowledge of constitutional law, made him a fit delegate to England in pleading the cause of the colony before the metropolitan authorities. His speech on the occasion is reported in the *Canadian Review*, published at Montreal, in 1826.

Colonel Hy. Caldwell states that, in 1775, Governor Guy Carleton had ordered a cannon to be pointed from the wharf on which stood Lymburner's house, with the intention to open fire upon the *Bostonais*, should they attempt a surprise on the *Sault-au-Matelot* quarter. Massive and strongly built stone vaults (probably of French origin,) are still extant beneath the house adjoining, to the south of this last, belonging to the heirs Atkinson.

On the site of the offices of Mr. McGie, stood in 1759, the warehouse of M. Perrault ; from a great number of of letters and invoice-bills found in the garret, and which a friend (3) has placed at our disposal, it would seem that M. Perrault had extensive commercial relations both in Canada and in France.

---

ed by the King, the 1st March, 1688. The 25th August, 1750, *Messire Christophe De Lalane, Directeur du Séminaire des Missions Etrangères à Paris*, made a concession of it to Mons. Nicholas René Levasseur, *Ingénieur*, formerly chief contractor of the ships of "His Most Christian Majesty." On the 24th June, 1760, a deed of sale of this same property, to Joseph Brassard Descheneaux, consisting of a two story house and a wharf (*avec les peintures au-dessus de la porte.*) On the 8th September, 1764, a deed of sale to Alexander McKenzie, purchase money, $5,800. On the 19th April, 1768, Joseph Descheneaux assigned his mortgage to Mr. John Lymburner. On the 11th August, 1781, a deed of concession of the beach in the rear, to low water mark, by the Seminary to Adam Lymburner. The 5th November, 1796, a deed of sale by the attorney of Adam Lymburner. Subsequently, Angus Shaw, became the proprietor in consideration of $4,100. On the 17th October, 1825, a judicial sale, to the late Henry Atkinson, Esq.

(3) Hon. D. A. Ross.

St. Peter street has become the general head-quarters of the most important commerce, life insurance and fire assurance offices. The financial institutions, are there, proudly enthroned : the Bank of Montreal, Bank of Quebec, the Union Bank, the *Banque Nationale*, the Stadacona Bank, the Bank of British North America, the Merchants' Bank.

In this street resided, in 1774, the Captain Bouchette who in the following year, in his little craft " Le Gaspé," brought us back our brave Governor, Guy Carleton ; M. Bouchard, merchant ; M. Panet, N.P., (the father of His Lordship, Bishop B. C. Panet), as also M. Boucher, harbor master of Quebec, "(who was appointed to that post by the Governor Sir R. S. Milnes, on the recommendation of the Duke of Kent)." Boucher had piloted the vessel, (having on board the 7th Regiment, the Duke's,) from Quebec to Halifax.

The office in which the *Quebec Morning Chronicle* has been published since 1847, belonged in 1759 to M. Jean Taché, "President of the Mercantile Body," " an honest and sensible man " as appears by *Mémoires sur le Canada*, (1749-60). One of our first poets, he composed a poem " On the Sea." He is the ancestor of the late Sir E. P. Taché, and of the novelist, Jos. Marmette, and others. He possessed, moreover, at that period, extensive buildings on the Napoleon wharf, which were destroyed by fire in 1845, and a house in the country, on the Ste. Foye road, afterwards called " Holland House," after Major Samuel Holland.

The *Chronicle* building, during nearly half a century, was a coffee house, much frequented by sea-faring men, known as the " Old Neptune " Inn. The effigy of the Sea-god, armed with his formidable Trident, placed over the main entrance, seemed to threaten the passers-by. We can remember, as yesterday, his colossal proportions. "Old Neptune"* has disappeared about thirty years back.

---

* See *Histoire de la Gazette de Québec*—Gérin, p. 24.

Parallel with St. Peter street, runs *Notre-Dame* street, which leads us to the little Church of the Lower Town, named *Notre-Dame de la Victoire*, in remembrance of the victory achieved in 1690, on the then besieger, Sir Wm. Phipps. This Church was, at a later period, called "*Notre-Dame des Victoires*," in commemoration of the dispersion by a storm of Admiral Walker's squadron, in 1711. The corner of these streets (St. Peter and Sous-le-Fort streets) is probably the site of the walks and garden plots where Champlain cultivated roses and carnations about the year 1615.

Fronting the Church of "*Notre-Dame des Victoires*" and on the site now occupied as Blanchard's Hotel, the Ladies of the *Ursulines*, in 1639, found a refuge in an humble residence, a sort of shop or store, owned at that period by the *Sieur Juchereau des Chatelets*, at the foot of the path (*sentier*), leading up to the mountain (foot of Mountain street), and where the then Governor, M. de Montmagny, as is related, sent them their first Quebec meal.

The locality possessed other traditions of agreeable memory ; the good, the youthful, the beautiful *Madame de Champlain*, about the year 1620, here catechised and instructed, under the shadow of the trees, the young Huron Indians in the principles of Christianity. History relates their surprise and joy on seeing their features reflected in the small mirror which their benefactress wore suspended at her side, according to the then prevailing custom.

In 1682, a conflagration broke out in the Lower Town which, besides the numerous vaults and stores, reduced into ashes a considerable portion of the buildings. At a later period "*Notre-Dame de la Victoire*" (Church) was built on part of the ruins. Let us open the second volume of the "*Cours d'Histoire du Canada*," by the *Abbé Ferland*, and let us read "Other ruins existed (in 1684) in the commercial centre of the Lower Town ; these ruins con-

sisted of blackened and delapidated walls. Champlain's
old warehouse which, from the hands of the Company
(" *Compagnie de la Nouvelle France*"), had passed in those
of the King (Louis XIV), had remained in the same state as
when left after the great fire which, some years previously,
had devastated the Lower Town."

In 1684, Monseigneur de Laval obtained this site or
*emplacement* from M. de la Barre for the purpose of erecting
a supplementary chapel for the use of the inhabitants in
the Lower Town. This gift, however, was ratified only
later, in favor of M. de St. Valier, in the month of
September, 1685. Messieurs de Denonville and de Meulles
caused a clear and plain title or patent of this locality to be
issued for the purpose of erecting a church which, in the
course of time, was built by the worthy Bishop and named
" *Notre-Dame de la Victoire.*" The landing for small craft,
in the vicinity of the old market (now the Finlay (1)
Market), was called " *La Place du Débarquement.*"

It is in this vicinity, (a little to the west.) under the
silent shade of a wood near the garden which Champlain
had laid out, that the historical interview, in 1608, which
saved the colony, took place. The secret was of the
greatest importance ;—it is not to be wondered at if
Champlain's trusty pilot, Captain Testu, deemed it proper
to conduct the founder of Quebec and privily draw him
aside, into the neighbouring wood and make known to him
the villanous plot which one of the accomplices, Antoine
Natel, locksmith, had first disclosed to him under the
greatest secrecy. The chief of the conspiracy was one Jean
du Val, who had come to the country with Champlain.

---

(1) William Finlay, an eminent merchant of Quebec, and one of its chief
benefactors, made several bequests which the City authorities invested in the
purchase of this market. Mr. Finlay died at the Island of Maderia, whether
he had gone for his health, about the year 1831.

In the early days of the colony, the diminutive market space, facing the front of *Notre-Dame* church, Lower Town, as well as the Upper Town Market, was used for the infliction of corporal punishment or the pillory, on culprits.

On the area facing the Lower Town church on Notre-Dame street, the Plan of the City, drawn by the Engineer, Jean Bourdon, in 1661, shows a bust of Louis XIV, long since removed; this market, which dates from the earliest times of the colony, as well as the vacant area (formerly the Upper Town market, facing the Basilica,) was used as a place for corporal punishment, and for the exhibition in the pillory of public malefactors. The *Quebec Gazette* of 19th June, 1766, mentions the whipping, on the Upper and Lower Town markets, of Catherine Berthrand and Janette Blaize, by the hand of the executioner, for having "borrowed" (a pretty way of describing petty larceny) a silver spoon from a gentleman of the town, without leave or without intention of returning it."

For male reprobates, such as Jean May and Louis Bruseau, whose punishment for petty larceny is noted in the *Gazette* of 11th August, 1766, the whipping was supplemented with a walk—tied at the cart's tail—from the Court House door to St. Roch and back to the Court House. May had to whip Bruseau and Bruseau had to whip May the day following, at ten in the morning.

Let us revert to Captain Testu's doings.

The plot was to strangle Champlain, pillage the warehouse and afterwards betake themselves to the Spanish and *Basques* vessels, lying at Tadousac. As, at that period, no Court of Appeals existed in *"la Nouvelle France"*—far less was a "Supreme Court" thought of—the trial of the chief of the conspiracy was soon despatched, says Champlain, and the Sieur Jean du Val was *"presto"* well and duly hanged "and strangled at Quebec aforesaid, and his head affixed to

" the top of a pike-staff planted on the highest eminence of
" the Fort." The ghastly head of this traitor, on the end
of a pike-staff, near *Notre-Dame* street, must certainly have
had a picturesque effect at twilight.

But the brave Captain Testu, saviour of Champlain and
of Quebec,—what became of him?—Champlain has done
him the honor of naming him; here the matter ended.
Neither monument, nor poem, nor page of history in his
honor; nothing was done in the way of commemorating his
devotion. As in the instance of the illustrious man, whose
life he had saved, his grave is unknown. According to
the Abbé Tanguay, none of his posterity exist at this day.

During the siege of 1759, we notice in *Panet's* Journal,
" that the Lower Town was a complete mass of smoking
ruins; on the 8th August, it was a burning heap (*brasier*).
Wolfe and Saunder's bombshells had found their way even
to the under-ground vaults. This epoch became disastrous
to many Quebecers." The English threw bombs (*pots à feu*)
on the Lower Town, of which, says Mr. Panet, "one fell on
my house, one on the houses in the Market-Place, and the
last in Champlain street. The fire burst out simultaneously,
in three different directions; it was in vain to attempt to
cut off or extinguish the fire at my residence; a gale was
blowing from the north-east and the Lower Town was
soon nothing less than a blazing mass. Beginning at my
house, that of M. Desery, that of M. Maillou, *Sault-au-Matelot*
street, the whole of the Lower Town and all the quarter
*Cul-de-Sac* up to the property of *Sieur Voyer*, which was
spared, in short up to the house of the said Voyer, the
whole was devastated by the fire. Seven vaults * had been

---

* The most spacious, the most remarkable of these substantial vaults of
French construction, are those which now belong to the Estate Poston on
the north side of Notre-Dame street, nearly opposite the church Notre-Dame
des Victoires. It is claimed that these vaults were so constructed as not
only to be fire-proof but water-proof likewise at the seasons of high water, in
spring and autumn. This vault is now occupied by Messrs. Thompson,
Codville & Co.

rent to pieces or burned : that of M. Perrault the younger, that of M. Taché, of M. Benjamin de la Mordic, of Jehaune, of Maranda. You may judge of the consternation which reigned ; 167 houses had been burnt."

One hundred and sixty-seven burnt houses would create many gaps. We know the locality on which stood the warehouse of M. Perrault, junior, also that of M. Taché (the *Chronicle Bureau*), but who can point out to us where stood the houses of Desery, Maillou, Voyer, de Voisy, and the vaults of Messieurs Turpin, de la Mordic, Jehaune, Maranda ?

It is on record that Champlain, after his return to Quebec in 1633, "had taken care to refit a battery which he had planted on a level with the river near the warehouse, the guns of which commanded the passage between Quebec and the opposite shore." (1) Now, in 1683, "this cannon battery, erected in the Lower Town, almost surrounded on all sides by houses, stood at some distance from the edge of the river and caused some inconvenience to the public ; the then Governor, *Lefebvre de la Barre* (2) having sought out a much more advantageous locality towards the Point of Rocks (*pointe des Roches*) west of the *Cul-de-Sac*, and on the margin of the said river at high-water mark, which would more efficiently command and sweep the harbour, and which would cause far less inconvenience to the houses in the said Lower Town," considered it fit to remove the said battery, and the Reverend Jesuit Fathers having proposed to contribute towards the expenses which would be incurred in so doing, he made them a grant "of a portion of the lot of ground (*emplacement*) situated in front of the site on which is now planted the said cannon battery, **** between the street or high road for wheeled

(1) "*Cours d'Histoire du Canada*," *Ferland*, Vol. 1, p. 280.
(2) *Concession de La Barre aux Jésuites*, 16 Sept. 1683.

vehicles coming from the harbour (3) and the so called Saint Peter street."

Here then we have the origin of the Napoleon wharf and a very distinct mention of Saint Peter street. The building erected near this site was sold on the 22nd October, 1763, to William Grant, esquire, who, on the 19th December, 1763, also purchased the remainder of the ground down to low-water mark, from Thomas Mills, esquire, Town Major, who had shortly before obtained a grant or patent of it, the 7th December, 1763, from Governor Murray, in recognition, as is stated in the preamble of the patent, of his military services. This property which, at a later period, belonged to the late William Burns, was by him conveyed, the 16th October, 1806, to the late J. M. Woolsey. The Napoleon wharf, purchased in 1842 by the late M. Julien Chouinard from the late M. Frs. X. Buteau, forms at present part of the Estate Chouinard ; in reality, it is composed of two wharves joined into one ; the western portion is named "The Queen's Wharf."

The highway which leads from the Cape towards this wharf is named "Sous-le-Fort" street, which sufficiently denotes its position ; this street, the oldest, probably, dates from the year 1620, when the foundations of Fort St. Louis were laid; we may presume that, in 1663, the street terminated at "la Pointe des Roches." In the last century, "Sous-le-Fort" street was graced by the residences, among others, of Fleury de la Jaunière, brother of Fleury de la Gorgendière, brother-in-law of the Governor de Vaudreuil.

In this street also stood the house of M. George Allsop, the head of the opposition in Governor Cramahé's Council,

(3) M. de Laval, in 1661, described the city as follows :

"Quebecum vulgo in superiorem dividitur et inferiorem urbem. In inferiore sunt portus, vadosa navium ora, mercatorum apotecae ubi et merces servantur, commercium quodlibet peragitur publicum et magnus civium numerus commoratur."

&c. His neighbor was M. D'Amours des Plaines, Councillor of the Superior Council; further on, stood the residence of M. Cuvillier, the father of the Honorable Austin Cuvillier, in 1844, speaker of the House of Assembly.

In this street also, existed the warehouse of M. Cugnet, the lessee of the Domaine of Labrador.

We must not confound the Napoleon Wharf with the Queen's Wharf, the property of the late J. W. Woolsey. From the King's Wharf to the King's forges (the ruins of which were discovered at the beginning of the century, a little further up than the King's store), there are but a few steps.

G. Bellet, M.P., resided on the property of Mr. Julien Chouinard, at the corner of St. Peter and *Sous-le-Fort* streets. In the space between the Queen's Wharf and the jetty on the west, belonging to the Imperial authorities and called the King's Wharf, there existed a bay or landing place, much prized by our ancestors, which afforded a harbour for the coasting vessels and small river-crafts, called the *"Cul-de Sac."* There also, the ships which were overtaken by an early winter, lingered until the sunny days of April released them from their icy fetters through the melting of the frozen masses born of the river. There the ships were put into winter-quarters, and securely bedded on a foundation or bed of clay; wrecked vessels also came hither to undergo repairs. The *Cul-de-Sac* with its uses and marine traditions, had, in bygone days, its usefulness in our incomparable sea-port. In this vicinity, Vaudreuil had, in 1759, planted a battery.

The Custom House (now the Department of Marine,) was built on this site in 1833. The *Cul-de-Sac* re-calls "the first chapel which served as a Parish Church at Quebec," that which Champlain caused to be built in the Lower Town in 1615, in the *Cul-de-Sac* bay, where the name of Champlain is identical with the street which was bounded by this

Chapel. The Revd. Fathers *Récollets* there performed their clerical functions up to the period of the taking of Quebec by the brothers Kertk, from 1615 to 1629, (Laverdière).

Nothing less than an urgent necessity to provide the public with a convenient market-place, and to the small coasting steamers, suitable wharves, could move the municipal authorities to construct the wharves now existing and there, in 1856, to erect out of the materials of the old Parliament House, the spacious Champlain Hall, so conspicuous at present. The King's Wharf and the King's stores, two hundred and fifty feet in length, with a guard house, built on the same site in 1821, possess also their marine and military traditions. The "Queen's Own" Volunteers, Capt. Rayside, were quartered there during the stirring times of 1837-8, when "Bob Symes" dreamed each night of a new conspiracy against the British Crown, and M. Aubin perpetuated, in the Ambrosia of his *"Fantasque,"* the memory of this loyal magistrate.

How many saucy frigates, how many proud English Admirals, have made fast their boats at the steps of this wharf ! Jacques Cartier, Champlain, Nelson, Bougainville, Cook, Vauclain, Montgomery, Boxer, have, one after the other, trodden over this picturesque landing place, commanded as it is by the guns of Cape Diamond. Since about a century, the street which bears the venerated name of the Founder of Quebec, *"Champlain"* street, unmindful of its ancient Gallic traditions, is almost exclusively the headquarters of our Hibernian population. An ominous looking black board, affixed to one of the projecting rocks of the Cape, indicates the spot below where one of their countrymen, Brigd. Gen. Richard Montgomery, with his two *Aides-de-Camp* Cheeseman and McPherson, received their death blow during a violent snow storm about five o'clock in the morning, the 31st December, 1775. On this disastrous morning, the Post was guarded by Canadian Militia men,

Messieurs Chabot and Picard. Captain Barnesfare, an English mariner, had pointed the cannon; Coffin and Sergeant Hugh McQuarters, applied the match. At the Eastern extremity under the stairs, now styled "Breakneck steps," according to Messrs. Casgrain and Laverdière, was discovered Champlain's Tomb, though a rival antiquary, M. S. Drapeau, says that he is not certain of this.*

A little to the west is *Cap Blanc*, inhabited by a small knot of French Canadians and some Irish; near by, was launched in October, 1750, the *Orignal*, a King's ship, built at Quebec; at that period, the lily flag of France floated over the bastions of Cape Diamond : the *Orignal*, in being launched, broke her back and sunk.

Champlain street stretches nearly to *Cap Rouge*, a distance of six miles. During the winter, the most marked incidents which take place, are : the fall of an avalanche from the brow of the Cape on the roofs of the houses beneath, occasionally carrying death in its train;—in good, former years, the laying of the keel of a large vessel in the ship-yards of Messrs. Gilmour, Dinning, Baldwin, &c. This brought joy to the heart of the poor ship-carpenters ; many of whose white, snug, cottages, are grouped along the river near by.

Except during the summer months, when the crews of the ships, taking in cargo alongside the booms, sing, fight and dance in the adjacent "shebeens," the year glides on peacefully. On grand, on gala-days, in election times, some of the sons of St. Patrick perambulate the historical street, flourishing treenails, or *shillaleghs*—in order to *preserve the peace ! ! !* of course. To sum up all, Champlain street has an aspect altogether *sui generis*.

---

* In fact, the spot where the remains of the great geographer and discoverer are supposed to rest, seems to be the site on which the new Post Office in the Upper Town has lately been built. Another theory, however, is lately propounded by an Ottawa antiquary. See QUEBEC PAST AND PRESENT.

Among the streets of Quebec, the most celebrated in our annals by reason of the incidents which attach thereto, one may name the frowsy and tortuous highway which circulates from the foot of Mountain hill, running for a distance of two hundred feet below the cape, up to the still narrower pathway which commences west of Saint James' street and leads to the foot of the hill "*de la canoterie* (1);" all will understand we mean *Sault-au-Matelot* street. Is it because a sailor no doubt partially relieved from the horrors of sobriety? or are we to attribute it to the circumstance of a dog named "*Matelot*" ("Sailor") there taking a leap (2)? Consult *Du Creux*. Our friend, Joseph Marmette appropriated it for the reception of his hero "*Dent de Loup*," who escaped without broken bones, after his leap. (3)

This still narrower pathway of which we have just spoken, rejoices in the name "*Ruelle des Chiens*" (Dog Lane): so it is called by the people; the Directories name it Dambourgès street or "*Petite rue Sault-au-Matelot*." It is so narrow that, at certain angles, two carts passing in opposite directions, would be blocked. Just picture to yourself that up to the period of 1816, our magnanimous ancestors had no other outlet in this direction at high water, to reach Saint Roch (for Saint Paul street was constructed subsequently to 1816, as M. de Gaspé has informed us.) Is it not incredible? As, in certain passes of the Alps, a watchman no doubt stood at either extremity of this pass, provided with a speaking trumpet, to give notice of any obstruction and thus prevent collisions. This

(1) The Jesuit Fathers were in the habit of fastening the painter of their canoes at the foot of the hill, "*la canoterie*," on their return by water from their farm called "*Ferme des Anges*," hence its name.

(2) Did the dog belong to Champlain, an antiquary asks us?

"Ad lævum fluit amnis St. Laurenti, ad dextram S. Caroli fluviolus.. Ad "confluentem, Promontorium assurgit, *Saltum Nautæ* vulgo vocant, ab canis "hujus nominis qui se alias ex eo loco præcipitem debit." (Historia Canadensis.—Creuzius, p. 204.)

(3) Françoise de Bienville.

odoriferous locality, especially during the dog-days, is rather densely populated. The babes of Green Erin, with a sprinkling of young *Jean Baptistes*, here flourish like rabbits in a warren.

Adventurous tourists who have risked themselves there in the sultry days of July, have found themselves dazed at sight of the wonders of the place. Among other indigenous curiosities, they have there noticed what might be taken for any number of aerial tents improvised no doubt as protection from the scorching rays of a meridian sun. Attached to ropes stretched from one side of the public-way to the other, was the family linen, hung out to dry. When shaken by the wind over the heads of the passers-by, these articles of white under-clothing, (*chemisettes*) flanked by sundry masculine nether-garments, presented a *tableau*, it is said, in the highest degree picturesque. As regards ourselves, desirous from our early days to search into the most recondite *arcana* of the history of our City and to portray them in all their suggestive reality, for the edification of distinguished tourists from England, France, and the United States, it has been to us a source of infinite mortification to realize that the only visit which we ever made to Dog-Lane was subsequent to the publication of the *Album du Touriste*; a circumstance which explains the omission of it from that repository of Canadian lore. Our most illustrious *tourists, the elder son of the Queen, the Prince of Wales,

---

* CANADA'S ROYAL VISITORS—WHO HAVE BEEN HERE SINCE 1787.

"Canada has been honored with visits from the following Royal personages :— His Royal Highness Prince William Henry (afterwards William IV), uncle of Her Majesty Queen Victoria, landed in Quebec in 1787. H. R. H. Prince Edward, Duke of Kent, father of Queen Victoria, visited Canada in 1791, four years later than his brother. H. R. H. Albert Edward, Prince of Wales and heir apparent of the British Crown, was in this country in 1860, and laid the corner-stone of the Parliament Buildings at Ottawa. H. R. H. Prince Alfred, Duke of Edinburgh, second son of Queen Victoria, was here in 1861. H. R. H. Prince de Joinville, son of Louis Philippe, once King of France, was in Canada the same year as Prince Alfred. Prince Napoleon Bonaparte, cousin of ex-Napoleon III, Emperor of France, also in 1861. H. R. H. Prince Arthur, third son of the Queen, in 1869. H. R. H. the Grand Duke Alexis of Russia, in 1871. H. R. H. Dom Pedro, Emperor of Brazil, in 1876 (Centennial year) ; and Her Royal Highness the Princess Louise and H. R. H. the Duke of Edinburgh (his second visit), in 1878. It will thus be seen that Queen Victoria's father, uncle and four of her children have been in Canada."

his brothers, the Princes Alfred and Arthur, the Dukes of Newcastle, and of Manchester, of Beaufort, of Argyle, Generals Grant and Sherman, and Prince Napoleon Bonaparte, it is said, took their leave of Quebec without having visited that interesting locality, "*la Ruelle des Chiens,*" probably unconscious of its very existence! Nevertheless, this street possesses great historical interest. It has re-echoed the trumpet sounds of war, the thundering of cannon, the briskest musketry ; there, fell Brigadier General Arnold, wounded in the knee: carried off amid the despairing cries of his soldiers reeking in gore, under the swords of Dambourgès, of the fierce and stalwart Charland, of the brave Caldwell, followed by his friend Nairn and their chivalrous militiamen. Our friends, the annexationists of that period, were so determined to annex Quebec, that they threw themselves as if possessed by the evil one, upon the barriers (there were two of them) of *la Ruelle des Chiens,* and in *Sault-au-Matelot street ;* each man (says Sanguinet) wearing a slip of paper on his cap on which was written "*Mors aut Victoria,*" "Death or Victory !" One hundred years and more have elapsed since this fierce struggle, and we are not yet under Republican rule ! !

A number of dead bodies lay in the vicinity, on the 31st December, 1775 ; they were carried to the Seminary. Ample details of the incidents of this glorious day will be found in "QUEBEC PAST AND PRESENT." It is believed that the first barrier was placed at the foot of the stone *demi-lune* where, at present, a cannon rests on the ramparts; the second was constructed in rear of the present offices of Mr. W. D. Campbell, N.P., in *Sault-au-Matelot* street.

*Sault-au-Matelot* street has lost the military renown which it then possessed ; apart from the offices of M. Ledroit, of the *Morning Chronicle,* of the Timber Cullers, it now is a stand for the carters; and a numerous tribe of coopers whose casks on certain days encumber the sidewalks.

Saint Paul street does not appear on the plan of the City of Quebec of 1660, reproduced by the Abbé Faillon. This quarter of the Lower Town so populous under the French *régime*, and where, according to Monsg. de Laval, there was in 1661, " *Magnus numerus civium*," continued, until about 1832, to represent by the hurry-scurry of affairs and the residences of the principal merchants, one of the wealthiest portions of the City. There, in 1793, the father of our Queen, Colonel of the 7th Fusileers, then in garrison at Quebec, partook of the hospitality of M. Lymburner, one of the merchant princes of that period. Was the *chère amie*, the elegant *Baronne de St. Laurent*, of the party? We found it impossible to ascertain this from our old friend Hon. William Sheppard, of Woodfield, near Quebec, (who died in 1867), from whom we obtained this incident. Mr. Sheppard, who had frequently been a guest at the most select drawing-rooms of the ancient capital, was himself a contemporary of the generous and jovial Prince Edward.

The *Sault-au-Matelot* quarter, Saint Peter street, Saint James' street, down to the year 1832, contained the habitations of a great number of persons in easy circumstances; many of our best families had their residences there. Evidences of the luxuriousness of their dwelling-rooms are visible to this day, in the pannelling of some doors and in decorated ceilings.

Drainage, according to the modern system, was, at that period, almost unknown to our good City. The Asiatic scourge, in 1832, decimated the population; 3,500 corpses, in the course of a few weeks, had gone to their last resting place. This terrible epidemic was the occasion, so to speak, of a social revolution at Quebec; the land on the St. Louis and Ste. Foye roads, became much enhanced in value; the wealthy quitted the Lower Town. Commercial affairs, however, still continued to be transacted there, but the residences of merchants were selected in the Upper Town, or in the country parts adjacent.

The *Fief Sault-au-Matelot*, which at present belongs to the Seminary, was granted to Guillaume Hébert, on the 4th February, 1623, the title of which was ratified by the Duke de Ventadour on the last day of February. 1632. On the ground reclaimed from the river, about 1815, Messrs. Munro and Bell, eminent merchants, built wharves and some large warehouses, to which lead " Bell's-lane " (so named after the Honorable Matthew Bell,) (1) the streets "Saint James," " Arthur," " Dalhousie " and others. Mr. Bell, at a later period, one of the lessees of the Saint Maurice Forges, resided in the tenement—St. Lawrence Chambers—situate at the corner of St. James and St. Peter streets, now belonging to Mr. John Greaves Clapham, N. P. Hon. Matthew Bell commanded a troop of cavalry, which was much admired by those warlike gentlemen of 1812—our respected fathers. He left a numerous family, and was related by marriage to the families Montizambert, Bowen, &c. Dalhousie street, in the Lower Town, probably dates from the time of the Earl of Dalhousie (1827), when the " Quebec Exchange " was built by a Company of Merchants. The extreme point of the Lower Town, towards the north-east, constitutes " *La Pointe à Carcy.*" In the offing, is situated the wharf alongside of which, the stately frigate " Aurora," Captain De Horsey, passed the winter of 1866-7. The wharves of the Quebec Docks now mark the spot.

The expansion of commerce at the commencement of the present century, and increase of population rendered it very desirable that means of communication should be established between the Lower Town and St. Roch, less rugged and inconvenient than the tunnel—Dog's Lane—and the sandy beach of the river St. Charles

(1) Opened by him in 1831.

at low water. Towards 1816, the northern extremity of St. Peter street was finished; it was previously bounded by a red bridge, well remembered by our very old citizens. The Apostle St. Paul was honored with a street, as was his colleague, St. Peter. Messrs. Benj. Tremaine, Budden, Morrisson, Parent, Allard and others, acquired portions of ground, on the north side of this (St. Paul) street, upon which they have erected wharves, offices and large warehouses. Renaud's new block now occupies a portion of the site.

The construction of the North Shore Railway will have the effect, at an early date, of augmenting, in a marked degree, the value of these properties, the greater portion of which now belong to our fellow citizen, M. J. Bte. Renaud, who has adorned this portion of the Lower Town with first class buildings. Let us hope that this quarter may flourish and that our enterprising fellow citizen may not suffer in consequence. (1)

## CHAP. V.

On emerging from St. Louis Gate, several handsome cut stone modern dwellings are noticeable; the second, Hon. Frs. Langelier's—close to Mr. Shehyn's. The Hamel Terrace is quite a credit to the new town. The New town outside of the walls, like that of New Edinburgh, in beauty and design will very soon cast the historical old town within the walls in the shade. The next object which attracts the eye is the

---

(1) We borrow from the "Directory for the City and Suburbs of Quebec," for 1791, by Hugh McKay, printed at the office of the *Quebec Herald*, the following paragraph, "*Rues Ecartées*" (out of the way streets.) "*La Canoterie* (Canoe Landings) follows the street *Sault-au-Matelot*, commencing "at the house of Cadet (where Mr. Ol. Aylwin resides) and continues up to "Mr. Grant's distillery; St. Charles street commences there and terminates "below Palace Gate; St. Nicholas street extends from Palace Gate to the "water's edge, passing in front of the residence of the widow La Vallée; the "old ship yard opposite to the boat yard; Cape Diamond street commences "at the wharf owned by Mr. Antrobus and terminates at the outer extremity "of that of Mons. Dumière underneath Cape Diamond; the streets *Carrière*, "*Mont-Carmel*, *Ste. Geneviève*, *St. Denis*, *Des Grisons*, are all situated above "St. Louis street." (Mr. Louis Dumière was M. P. in 1828.)

spacious structure of the Skating Rink, the only charge we
can make against it, is that it is too close to St. Louis Gate.
'Tis the right thing in the wrong place.   Adjoining stood
the old home of the Prentices, in 1791,—Bandon Lodge,*
once the abode of Sandy Simpson,† whose cat-o'nine-tails
must have left lively memories in Wolfe's army.   Did the
beauteous damsel about whom Horatio, Lord Nelson, rave
in 1782, when, as Commander of H. M.'s frigate *Albemarle*,
he was philandering in Quebec, ever live here?‡   This is
more than I can say.   On the north side of the *Grande Allée*,
the lofty structure—the new Parliament Buildings—
occupies a whole square.   Opposite looms out the long tea-
caddy-looking building, built by the Sandfield Macdonald
government in 1862,—the Volunteer Drill Shed.   Its length,
if not its beauty, attracts notice.   "Ferguson's house," next
it, noted by Professor Silliman in his "*Tour between Hart-
ford and Quebec in* 1819," is now difficult to recognize; its
present owner, A. Joseph, Esq., has added so much to its
size.   This antiquated dwelling certainly does not belong
to the new dispensation.   Another land-mark of the past
deserves notice—the ex-Commander§ of the Forces' lofty
quarters; from their angular eaves and forlorn aspect, they
generally went by the name of "Bleak House."   I cannot
say whether the place ever was haunted, but it ought to
have been.*   On the summit of the plateau, formerly known
as *Buttes à Nepveu*, and facing Mr. John Roche's stately
mansion, Hon. P. Garneau has constructed another handsome terrace of cut stone dwellings.   We are now in the

* The residence of Jos. Shehyn, Esq., M.P.P., occupies now this historic site.

† SAUNDERS SIMPSON.—Ho was Prevost Marshall in Wolfe's army, at the affairs of Louisbourg, Quebec and Montreal, and cousin of my father's.   He resided in that house, the nearest to St. Louis Gate, outside, which has not undergone any external alteration since I was a boy."—*From unpublished Diary of Deputy Commissary General Jas. Thompson.*

‡ Recent evidence extracted by Dr. H. H. Miles out of Jas. Thompson's papers and letters, lead to strengthen the theory previously propounded, and to indicate Miss Mary Simpson, daughter of Saunders Simpson, as the famed Quebec beauty of 1782.

§ Col. Durnford, Galway and others.

* Paint and extensive repairs have very much improved the historical house—this year tenanted by George Stewart, jr., Esq., author of *Lord Dufferin's Rule in Canada,*" "*The Great St. John's Fire,* 1877," &c.

*Grande Allée*—the forest avenue, which two hundred years ago led to Sillery Wood. On turning and looking back as you approach Bleak House, you have an excellent view of the Citadel, and of the old French works which extend beyond it, to the extremity of the Cape, overlooking *l'Anse des Mères.* A little beyond the Bleak House, at the top of what is generally known as Perrault's Hill, stands the Perrault† homestead, dating back to 1820, *l'Asyle Champêtre,*—now tastefully renovated and owned by Henry Dinning, Esq. The adjoining range of heights, occupied by the Martello Towers, the Garneau Terrace, &c., are known as the *Buttes à Nepveu.* " It was here that Murray took his stand on the morning of April 28th, 1760, to resist the advance of Levis, and here commenced the hardest-fought—the bloodiest action of the war, which terminated in the defeat of Murray, and his retreat within the city. The Martello Towers are bomb-proof, they are four in number, and form a chain of forts extending along the ridge from the St. Lawrence to the River St. Charles. The fact that this ridge commanded the city, unfortunately induced Murray to leave it and attempt to fortify the heights, in which he was only partially successful, owing to the frost being still in the ground.

The British Government were made aware of the fact, and seeing that from the improved artillery, the city was now fully commanded from the heights, which are about seven hundred yards distant, decided to build the Towers. Arrangements were accordingly made by Col. Brock, then commanding the troops in Canada. In 1806, the necessary materials were collected, and in the following year their construction commenced. They were not, however completed till 1812. The original estimate for the four was £8,000, but before completion the Imperial government had expended nearly £12,000. They are not all of the same

---

† Major Perrault and his esteemed father, the Prothonotary, a warm friend to education, both lived there many years.

size, but like all Martello Towers, they are circular and
bomb-proof. The exposed sides are *thirteen* feet thick and
gradually diminish like the horns of the crescent moon, to
*seven* feet in the centre of the side next the city walls. The
first or lower story contains tanks, storerooms and magazine ;
the second has cells for the garrison, with port-holes for
two guns. On the top there used to be one 68-pounder
carronade, two 24, and two 9-pounders."

A party of Arnold's soldiers ascended these heights in
November, 1775, and advanced quite close to the city walls,
shouting defiance at the little garrison. A few shots soon
dispersed the invaders, who retraced their steps to Wolfe's
Cove. On the *Buttes-à-Nepveu,* the great criminals were
formerly executed. Here, La Corriveau, the St. Valier La-
farge, met her deserved fate, in 1763, after being tried by
one of Governor Murray's Court Marshalls for murdering
her husband. After death she was hung in chains, or
rather in a solid iron cage, at the fork of four roads, at Levi,
close to the spot where the Temperance monument has
since been built. The loathsome form of the murderess
caused more than one shudder amongst the peaceable pea-
santry of Levi, until some brave young men, one dark night,
cut down the horrid cage, and hid it deep under ground,
next to the cemetery at Levi. where close to a century afterwards, it was dug up and sold to Barnum's agent for his
museum.

Sergeant Jas. Thompson describes in his diary, under
date 18th Nov., 1782, another memorable execution :

" This day two fellows were executed for the murder
and robbery of Capt. Stead, commander of one of the Treasury Brigs, on the evening of the 31st Dec., 1779, between
the Upper and Lower Town. The criminals went through
Port St. Louis, about 11 o'clock, at a slow and doleful pace,
to the place where justice had allotted them to suffer the
most ignominious death. It is astonishing to see what a

crowd of people followed the tragic scene. Even our people on the works (Cape Diamond) prayed Capt. Twiss for leave to follow the hard-hearted crowd." It was this Capt. Twiss who subsequently furnished the plan and built a temporary citadel in 1793.

In 1793, we have also recorded in history, another doleful procession of red coats, the Quebec Garrison, accompanying to the same place of execution a messmate (Draper), a soldier of the Fusileers, then commanded by the young Duke of Kent, who, after pronouncing the sentence of death, as commander, over the trembling culprit, kneeling on his coffin, as son and representative of the Sovereign, exercised the royal perogative of mercy and pardoned poor Draper.

Look down Perrault's hill towards the south. There stands, with a few shrubs and trees in the foreground, the Military Home,—where infirm soldiers, their widows and children, could find a refuge. It has recently been purchased and converted into the "Female Orphan Asylum." It forms the eastern boundary of a large expanse of verdure and trees, reaching the summit of the lot originally intended by the Seminary of Quebec for a Botanical Garden; subsequently it was contemplated to build their new seminary there to afford the boys abundance of fresh air. Alas! other counsels prevailed.

Its western boundary is a road leading to the new District Jail,—a stone structure of great strength, surmounted with a diminutive tower, admirably adapted, one would imagine, for astronomical pursuits. From its glistening cupola, Commander Ashe's Provincial Observatory is visable to the east.

I was forgetting to notice the substantial building, dating from 1855—the Ladies' Home. The Protestant Ladies of Quebec have here, at no small expense and trouble, raised a useful asylum, where the aged and infirm may find shelter. This, and the building opposite, St. Bridget's Asylum, with its growing fringe of trees and green plots, are decided ornaments to the *Grande Allée.*

The old burying ground of 1832, with all its ghastly memories of the Asiatic scourge, has assumed quite an ornate, nay a respectable aspect. Close to the toll-bar on the *Grande Allée,* may yet be seen one of the meredian stones which serve to mark the western boundary of the city, beyond the Messrs. Lampson's Mansion. On the adjoining domain, well named "Battlefield Cottage," formerly the property of Col. Charles Campbell, now owned by Michael Connolly, Esq., was the historic well out of which a cup of water was obtained to moisten the parched lips of the dying hero, James Wolfe, on the 13th Sept., 1759. The well was filled in a few years ago, but not before it was nigh proving fatal to Col. Campbell's then young son,—(Arch. Campbell, Esq., of Thornhill.) Its site is close to the western boundary fence, in the garden behind "Battlefield Cottage." Here we are at those immortal plains—the Hastings and Runnymeade of the two races once arrayed in battle against one another at Quebec. The western boundary of the Plains is a high fence enclosing Marchmont for years, the cherished family seat of John Gilmour, Esq., now occupied by Col. Fred. Turnbull, of the Canadian Hussars.

On the north-east corner of the Belvidere Road, may be seen a range of glass houses, put up by J. Doig, formerly gardener at Benmore.

A few minutes more brings the tourist to M. Price's villa, Wolfe-field, where may be seen the precipitous path up the St. Denis burn, by which the Highlanders and British soldiers gained a footing above, on the 13th September, 1759, and met in battle array to win a victory destined to revolutionize the New World. The British were piloted in their ascent of the river by a French prisoner brought with them from England—Denis de Vitré, formerly a Quebecer of distinction. Their landing place at Sillery was selected by Major Robert Stobo, who had, in May, 1759, escaped from a French prison in Quebec, and joined his countrymen, the English, at Louisbourg, from whence he took ship again to meet Admiral Saunders' fleet at Quebec. The tourist next drives past Thornhill, for years owned by Arch. Campbell, Esq., P. S. C., Sir Francis Hinck's old home, when Premier to Lord Elgin: opposite appear the leafy glades of Spencer Wood, so grateful a summer retreat, that my Lord used to say, " There he not only loved to live, but would like to rest his bones." Next comes Spencer Grange, the seat of J. M. LeMoine, Esq.; then Woodfield, the homestead of the Hon. Wm. Sheppard* in 1847, later on of Messrs. John Lawson and Jas. Gibb.† Facing the Woodfield property, on the Gomin Road, are visible the extensive Vineries and Peach Houses of Hon. Geo. Okill Stuart, Judge of the Vice-Admiralty Court. The eye next dwells on the rustic Church of St. Michael, embowered in evergreens; south of which looms out, at *Sous les Bois*, the stately convent of *Jésus-Marie ;* on the edge of the bank, to the south-east, at *Pointe-à-Pizeau*, stands the R. C. Church of St. Colomb de Sillery, in a most commanding position; on the Sillery heights, north-west of the Church of St. Michael, the late Bishop George J. Mountain owned a delightful summer retreat, recently sold to Albert H. Furniss, Esq.; then you meet with villas innumerable— one of the most conspicuous is Benmore, Col. Rhodes' country seat. Benmore is well worthy of a call, were it only to procure a *bouquet.* This is not merely the Eden of roses; Col. Rhodes has combined the farm with the garden. His underground rhubarb and mushroom cellars, his

---

* My old friend died in 1867—regretted as a scholar, an antiquarian and the type of the old English gentleman.

† This realm of fairy land, so rich in nature's graces, so profusely embellished by the late James Gibb, Esq., President of the Quebec Bank, was recently sold for a rural cemetery.

boundless asparagus beds and strawberry plantations, are a credit to Quebec.

Next come Clermont,‡ Beauvoir,|| Kilmarnock§, Cataraqui,** Kilgraston, Kirk-Ella,†† Meadow Bank,‡‡ Ravenswood,|||| Dornald,† until, after, a nine miles' drive, Redclyffe closes the rural landscape—Redclyffe,§§ on the top of *Cap Rouge* promontory. There, many indications yet mark the spot where Roberval's ephemeral colony wintered as far back as 1542. You can now, if you like, return to the city by the same route, or select the St. Foye Road, skirting the classic heights where General Murray, six months after the first battle of the Plains, lost the second, on the 2ҙth April, 1760; the St. Foye Church was then occupied by the British soldiers. Beauséjour is a beautiful demesne, where M. Ls. Bilodeau has several reservoirs, for the propagation of trout. Your gaze next rests on Holland House, Montgomery's headquarters in 1775, behind which is Holland Tree, overshadowing, as of yore, the grave of the Hollands.*

The view, from the St. Foye road, of the gracefully meandering St. Charles below, especially during the high tides, is something to be remembered. The tourist shortly after detects the iron pillar, surmounted by a bronze statue of Bellona, presented in 1855 by Prince Napoleon Bonaparte —intended to commemorate the fierce struggle at this spot

‡ The stately home of Thomas Beckett, Esq.

|| The picturesque villa of R. R. Dobell, Esq.

§ A mossy old hall founded by Mr. McNider in the beginning of the century; now occupied by the Graddon family.

** The gorgeous mansion of Chas. E. Levey, Esq.

†† The highly cultivated farm and summer residence of Andrew Stuart, Esq.

‡‡ The property of John Burstall, Esq.

|||| The beautiful home of W. Herring, Esq.

† The rustic abode of the late Hon. John Neilson, now owned by his son.

§§ Recently acquired by James Bowen, Esq., founded by the late W. Atkinson, Esq., in 1820.

* For account of the duel, which laid low one of the Hollands, see *Maple Leaves* for 1863. The tree, however, has lately been destroyed by a storm.

on the 28th April, 1760. In close vicinity, appear the bright *parterres* or umbrageous groves of *Bellevue*,† Hamwood, ‡ Bijou,‖ Westfield,§ *Sans-Bruit*, and the narrow gothic arches of Finlay Asylum ; soon you re-enter by St. John's Suburbs, with the broad basin of the St. Charles and the pretty Island of Orleans staring you in the face.

The principal objects to be noted in this street are : on the north side, St. John's Church, built in 1848—a large but not very elegant temple of R. C. worship, capable of seating 2,000 persons ; on the south side, St. Matthew's Church, (Church of England,) a handsome structure, whose beginnings, in 1828, were associated with the late Bishop G. J. Mountain's ministrations and munificence. The exertions of the Rev. Chs. Hamilton and the generous bequests of his brother, Robert Hamilton, and other members of the family, have been mainly instrumental in enlarging and decorating this building. Close by, is the new French Protestant Church. We shall close this short sketch with a mention of the "Quebec Protestant Burying Ground," originally bought by the Government of the Province of Quebec, from the heirs St. Simon, partly on the 9th December, 1771, and partly on the 22nd August, 1778. In the year 1823, Lord Dalhousie made a grant of this ground to the " Trustees of the Protestant Burying Ground," in whose hands it has remained until the 19th May, 1860, when the cemetery was declared closed by the 23rd Vict., chap. 70. Major Thomas Scott, Pay-master of the 70th Regiment, a brother to Sir Walter, was buried here in 1823. Major Thomas Scott was at one time charged with having written "ROB ROY." And next to St. John's Gate, looms out the handsome new building of the Y. M. C. Association, facing the new Montcalm Market.

---

† A stately Convent of Congregational Nuns.

‡ The ornate country seat of Robt. Hamilton, Esq.

‖ The cosy dwelling of And. Thompson, President Union Bank.

§ The homestead of Hon. D. A. Ross, late Atty.-Genl., Province of Quebec.

# SPENCER WOOD.

(By J. M. LeMoine.)

Through thy green groves and deep receding bowers,
Loved Spencer Wood! how often have I strayed,
Or mused away the calm, unbroken hours,
Beneath some broad oak's cool, refreshing shade.
—ADAM KIDD.*

On the South side of the St. Louis road, past Wolfe and Montcalm's famed battle-field, two miles from the city walls, lies, embowered in verdure, the most picturesque domain of Sillery—one might say of Canada—Spencer Wood.

---

* We give here the whole of the poetical tribute paid by Adam Kidd to a spot where he appears to have spent many happy hours, as a guest of the Percevals, together with his notes to the poem:—

### SPENCER WOOD.

Through thy green groves and deep receding bowers,
Loved Spencer Wood! how often have I strayed,
Or mused away the calm, unbroken hours,
Beneath some broad oak's cool, refreshing shade.

There, not a sound disturbed the tranquil scene,
Save welcome hummings of the roving bee,
That quickly flitted over the tufted green,
Or where the squirrel played from tree to tree.

And I have paused beside that dimpling stream,
Which slowly winds thy beauteous groves among,
Till from its breast retired the sun's last beam,
And every bird had ceased its vesper song.

The blushing arbors of those classic days,
Through which the breathings of the slender reed,
First softly echoed with Arcadia's praise,
Might well be pictured in this sheltered mead.

And blest were those who found a happy home
In thy loved shades, without one throb of care—
No murmurs heard, save from the distant foam
That rolled in columns o'er the great Chaudière. (1)

And I have watched the moon in grandeur rise
Above the tinted maple's leafy breast,
And take her brilliant pathway through the skies,
Till half the world seemed lulled in peaceful rest.

---

(1) "The Falls of the Chaudière are about nine miles from Quebec, on the south shore of the St. Lawrence, and for beauty and romantic scenery, perhaps not surpassed in all America. They are not so magnificent as Niagara, but certainly far more picturesque."

This celebrated Vice-Regal Lodge was (1780-96) known as Powell Place, when owned by General Henry Watson Powell; it took its name of Spencer Wood from the Right Honorable Spencer Perceval,* the illustrious relative of the Hon. Michael Henry Perceval, whose family possessed it from 1815 to 1833, when it was sold to the late Henry Atkinson, Esquire, an eminent and wealthy Quebec merchant. Hon. Mr. Perceval, member of the Executive and Legislative Council, had been H. M.'s Collector of Customs at Quebec for many years and until his death, which took place at sea, 12th October, 1829. The Percevals lived for many years in affluence in this sylvan retreat. Of their elegant receptions Quebecers still cherish pleasant reminiscences.† Like several royal villas of England and France, Spencer Wood had its periods of splendor alternated by

---

Oh! there were hours whose soft enchanting spell
Came o'er the heart, in thy grove's deep recess,
Where e'en poor Shenstone might have loved to dwell,
Enjoying the pure balm of happiness!

But soon, how soon, a different scene I trace,
Where I have wandered, or oft musing stood;
And those whose cheering looks enhanced the place,
No more shall smile on thee, lone Spencer Wood! (2)

---

(2) "This is one of the most beautiful spots in Lower Canada, and the property (1830) of the late Hon. Michael Henry Perceval, who resided there with his accomplished family, whose highly cultivated minds rendered my visits to Spencer Wood doubly interesting. The grounds and grand walks are tastefully laid out, interspersed with great variety of trees, planted by the hand of nature. The scenery is altogether magnificent, and particularly towards the east, where the great precipices overhang Wolfe's Cove. This latter place has derived its name from that hero, who, with his British troops, nobly ascended its frowning cliffs on the 13th September, 1759, and took possession of the Plains of Abraham."—ADAM KIDD, 1830.

(The HURON CHIEF and other Poems—ADAM KIDD.)

* The illustrious Chancellor of the Exchequer, Spencer Perceval, assassinated by Bellingham on the 11th May, 1812, probably took the name of Spencer from the Earls of Egmont and Northampton, connected with the Percevals.

† A Quebec lady writes to the Q. MORNING CHRONICLE:—"The once beautiful and accomplished Mrs. M. H. Perceval is no more! She died on the 23rd November, 1876, at Lews Castle, Stornoway, Scotland, at the residence of her son-in-law, Sir James Mathieson, deeply regretted by a large circle of friends, aged 86. At the age of 18 she was Acting Lady Mayoress of London, as her father, Sir Charles Flower, Lord Mayor, was a widower. At 19, she married the Hon. M. H. Perceval, who was appointed Collector of Customs in Quebec. They bought Powell Place, and gave it the name of Spencer Wood, after Earl Spencer, brother of Mr. Perceval. Their eldest son, Colonel of the Coldstream Guards, is also called Spencer; the Earl Spencer was his godfather. Few now remain to remember the splendid receptions given by the lovely and graceful Mrs. Perceval at Spencer Wood."—(MORNING CHRONICLE, 30th December, 1876.)

days of loneliness and neglect, short though they were. Spencer Wood, until 1849, comprised the adjoining property of Spencer Grange. Mr. Atkinson that year sold the largest half of his country seat—Spencer Wood—to the Government, as a gubernatorial residence for the hospitable and genial Earl of Elgin, reserving the smaller half (now owned by the writer) on which he built conservatories, vineries, a pinery and orchid house, &c., far more extensive than those of Spencer Wood proper. Though the place was renowned for its magnificence and princely hospitality in the days of Lord Elgin, there are amongst the living plenty to testify to the fact that the lawns, walks, gardens and conservatories were never kept up with the same intelligent taste and lavish expenditure as they were during the sixteen years (1833-1849) when this country seat owned for its master Henry Atkinson.

Spencer Wood garden is described in Loudon's *Encyclopedia of Gardening*, page 341, and also in the *Gardener's Magazine* for 1837, at page 467. Its ornate style of culture, which made it a show-place for all strangers visiting Quebec, was mainly due to the scientific and tasty arrangements of an eminent landscape gardener, M. P. Lowe, now in charge of the Cataraqui conservatories.

Well can we recall the time when this lordly demesne extended from Wolfefield, adjoining Marchmont, to the meandering Belle-Borne brook, which glides past the porter's lodge at Woodfield, due west : the historic stream *Ruisseau Saint Denis*, up which clambered the British hero, Wolfe, to conquer or die, intersecting it at Thornhill. It was then a splendid old seat of more than one hundred acres, a fit residence for the proudest nobleman England might send us as Vice-Roy—enclosed east and west between two streamlets, hidden from the highway by a dense growth of oak, maple, dark pines and firs—the forest primeval—letting in here and there the light of heaven on its labyrinthine avenues ; a most striking landscape, blend-

ing the sombre verdure of its hoary trees with the soft
tints of its velvety sloping lawn, fit for a ducal palace. An
elfish plot of a flower garden, alas! how much dwarfed,
then stood in rear of the dwelling to the north; it once
enjoyed the privilege of attracting many eyes. It had also
an extensive and well-kept fruit and vegetable garden,
enlivened with flower beds, the centre of which was
adorned with the loveliest possible circular fount in white
marble, supplied with the crystal element from the Belle-
Borne rill by a hidden aqueduct; conservatories, graperies,
peach and forcing houses, pavilions picturesquely hung
over the yawning precipice on two headlands, one looking
towards Sillery, the other towards the Island of Orleans,
the scene of many a cosy tea-party; bowers, rustic chairs
*perdues* among the groves, a superb bowling green and
archery grounds. The mansion itself contained an exquisite
collection of paintings from old masters, a well-selected
library of rare and standard works, illuminated Roman
missals, rich portfolios with curious etchings, marble
busts, quaint statuettes, medals and medallions, *objets de
vertu* purchased by the millionaire proprietor during a four
year's residence in Italy, France, and Germany; such we
remember Spencer Wood in its palmiest days, when it was
the ornate home of a man of taste, the late Henry Atkinson,
esquire, the President of the Horticultural Society of
Quebec.

In the beginning of the century Spencer Wood, as previously stated, was known as Powell Place. His Excellency Sir James Henry Craig spent there the summers of
1808-9-10. Even the healthy air of Powell Place failed to
cure him of gout and dropsy. A curious letter from
Sir James to his secretary and *charge d'affaires* in London,
H. W. Ryland, Esquire, dated "Powell Place, 6th August,
1810," has been, among others, preserved by the historian
Robert Christie. It alludes in rather unparliamentary language to the *coup d'état* which had on the 19th March, 1810,

consigned to a Quebec dungeon three of the most prominent members of the Legislature, Messrs. Bedard, Taschereau and Blanchet, together with Mr. Lefrançois, the printer of the *Canadien* newspaper, for certain comments in that journal, on Sir James' colonial policy. Sir James had spent the greatest part of his life in the army, actively battling against France; a Frenchman for him was a traditional enemy. This unfortunate idea seems more than once to have inspired his colonial policy with regard to the descendants of Frenchmen whom he ruled.

Born at Gibraltar, of Scotch parents, James Henry Craig entered the English service in 1763 at the age of 15, and on many occasions distinguished himself by his courage. During the war of the American revolution he served in Canada, and was present at the unfortunate affair of Saratoga.

### SIR JAMES CRAIG TO MR. RYLAND.

QUEBEC, Powell Place, 6th August, 1810.

My Dear Ryland,—Till I took my pen in my hand I thought I had a great deal to say to you, and now I am mostly at a loss for a subject. * * * We have remained very quiet; whatever is going on is silently. I have no reason to think, however, that any change has taken place in the public mind; *that* I believe remains in the same state. Bishop Plessis, on the return from his tour, acknowledged to me that he had reason to think that some of his *curés* had not behaved quite as they ought to have done; he is now finishing the remainder of his visitations.

Blanchette and Taschereau are both released on account of ill-health; the former is gone to Kamouraska to bathe, the latter was only let out a few days ago. He sent to the Chief Justice (Sewell,) to ask if he would allow him to call on him, who answered, by all means. The Chief Justice is convinced he is perfectly converted. He assured him that he felt it to be his duty to take any public occasion, by any act whatever that he could point out, to show his contrition and the sense he entertained of his former conduct.

He told the Chief Justice in conversation that Blanchette came and consulted him on the subject of publishing the paper, "Prenez vous par le bout du nez," and that having agreed that it would be very improper that it should appear, they went to Bedard, between whom and Blanchette there were very high words on the occasion. I know not what Panet is about, I have never heard one word of or about him. In short, I really have nothing to tell you, nor do I imagine that I shall have, till I hear from you. You may suppose how anxious I shall be till that takes place. We have fixed the time for about the 10th September; till then I shall not come to any final resolution with respect to the bringing the three delinquents to trial or not. I am, however, inclined to avoid it, so is the B——; the C. J. is rather, I think, inclined to the other side, though aware of the inconvenience that may arise from it. Blanchette and Taschereau have both, in the most unequivocal terms, acknowledged the criminality of their conduct, and it will be hinted that if Bedard will do the same it may be all that will be required of them; at present his language is that he has done nothing wrong, and that he does not care how long he is kept in prison.

We have begun upon the road to the townships (the Craig Road, through the Eastern Townships.) * * * We shall get money enough, especially as we hope to finish it at a third of what it would have cost if we would have employed the country people. (It was made by soldiers.)

The scoundrels of the Lower Town have begun their clamor already, and I shall scarcely be surprised if the House should ask, when they meet, by what authority I have cut a road without their permission. The road begins at St. Giles and will end at the township of Shipton.

Yours most faithfully,

(Signed,)  J. H. CRAIG.

(History of Canada, Christie, vol. VI., p. 128.)

Very different, and we hope more correct, views are now promulgated on colonial matters from Powell Place.

If Sir James, wincing under bodily pain, could write angry letters, there were occasions on which the "rank and fashion" of the city received from him the sweetest epistles imaginable. The 10th August of each year, (his birth-day perhaps) as he informs us in another letter, was sacred to rustic enjoyment, conviviality and the exchange of usual courtesies, which none knew better how to dispense than the sturdy old soldier.

The English traveller, John Lambert, thus notices it in his interesting narrative in 1808:—"Sir James Craig resided in summer at a country house about four or five miles from Quebec, and went to town every morning to transact business. This residence is called Powell Place, and is delightfully situated in a neat plantation on the border of the bank which overlooks the St. Lawrence, not far from the spot where General Wolfe landed and ascended to the heights of Abraham. Sir James gave a splendid breakfast *al fresco* at this place in 1809 to all the principal inhabitants of Quebec, and the following day he allowed his servants and their acquaintances to partake of a similar entertainment at his expense."—(Lambert's Travels, 1808, p. 310.)

12

Our late octogenarian friend, P. A. De Gaspé, esquire, an
eye-witness, describes one of these annual gatherings with
all the fervor of a youthful lover *

---

\* A *fête champêtre* AT POWELL PLACE IN 1809.

(From the French of P. A. DeGaspé.)

---

" Sir William Vivian, all a summer's day
Gave his broad lawns until the set of sun
Up to the people........................................"

(THE PRINCESS, *Tennyson*.)

" At half-past eight A. M., on a bright August morning, (I say a bright one,
for such had lighted up this welcome *fête champêtre* during three consecutive years)
the *élite* of the Quebec *beau monde* left the city to attend Sir James Craig's kind
invitation. Once opposite Powel Place (now Spencer Wood) the guests left their
vehicles on the main road, and plunged into a dense forest, following a serpentine
avenue which led to a delightful cottage in full view of the majestic Saint Lawrence ;
the river here appears to flow past, amidst luxuriant, green bowers which line its
banks. Small tables for four, for six, for eight guests are laid out, facing the cottage,
on a platform of *planed* deals—this will shortly serve as a dancing floor *al fresco ;*
as the guests successively arrive, they form in parties to partake of a *déjeuner en
famille.* I say *en famille* for an *aide-de-camp* and a few waiters excepted, no one
interferes with the small groups clubbed together to enjoy their early repast, of
which cold meat, radishes, bread, tea and coffee form the staples. Those whose
appetite is appeased make room for new comers, and amuse themselves strolling
under the shade of trees. At ten the cloth is removed ; the company are all on the
*qui vive.* The cottage, like the enchanted castle in the opera of Zemira and Azor,
only awaits the magic touch of a fairy ; a few minutes elapse, and the chief entrance
is thrown open ; little King Craig, followed by a brilliant staff, enters. Simultaneously
an invisible orchestra, located high amidst the dense foliage of large trees, strikes up
*God save the King.* All stand uncovered, in solemn silence, in token of respect to the
national anthem of Great Britain.

" The magnates press forward to pay their respects to His Excellency. Those
who do not intend to "trip the light fantastic toe" take seats on the platform
where His Excellency sits in state ; an A.D.C. calls out, *gentlemen, take your partners,*
and the dance begins.

" Close on sixty winters have run by since that day, when I, indefatigable
dancer, figured in a country dance of thirty couples. My footsteps, which now seem
to me like lead, scarcely then left a trace behind them. All the young hearts who
enlivened this gay meeting of other days, are mouldering in their tombs ; even *she*
the most beautiful of them all, *la belle des belles*—she, the partner of my joys and of
my sorrows—she, who on that day accepted in the circling dance, for the first time,
this hand. which two years after, was to lead her to the hymeneal altar—yes, even
she has been swept away by the tide of death.‡ May not I also say, with Ossian,
" ' Why art thou sad, son of Fingal ! Why grows the cloud of thy soul ! The sons
" of future years shall pass away ; another race shall arise ! The people are like the
" waves of the ocean ; like the leaves of woody Morven—they pass away in the
" rustling blast, and other leaves lift their green heads on high.' "

‡ Mr. DeGaspé married in 1811, Susanna, daughter of Thos. Allison, Esq., a
captain of the 6th Regiment, infantry, and of Therese Baby ; the latter's two brother
officers, Captain Ross Lewin and Bellingham, afterwards Lord Bellingham, married
at Detroit, then forming part of Upper Canada, two sisters, daughters of the Hon.
Jacques Duperon Baby.

Spencer Wood has ever been a favorite resort for our Governors—Sir James Craig—Lord Elgin—Sir Edmund Walker Head—Lord Monk—Lord Lisgar, and Lord Dufferin on his arrival in 1872; none prized it so highly, none rendered it more attractive than the Earl of Elgin. Of his *fêtes champêtres*, *recherchés* dinners, *château* balls, a pleasant remembrance still lingers in the memory of many Quebecers and others. Several circumstances added to the charms and comfort of Spencer Wood in his day. On one side of St. Louis Road, stood the gubernatorial residence; on the opposite side at Thornhill, dwelt the Prime Minister, Sir Francis Hincks. Over the vice-regal "walnuts and wine," how many knotty state questions have been discus-

---

"After all, why, indeed, yield up my soul to sadness? The children of the coming generation will pass rapidly, and a new one will take its place. Men are like the surges of the ocean; they resemble the leaves which hang over the groves of my manor; autumnal storms cause them to fall, but new and equally green ones each spring, replace the fallen ones. Why should I sorrow? Eighty-six children, grandchildren and great-grand-children, will mourn the fall of the old oak, when the breath of the Almighty shall smite it. Should I have the good fortune to find mercy from the sovereign judge; should it be vouchsafed to me to meet again the angel of virtue, who cheered the few happy days I passed in this vale of sorrow, we will both pray together for the numerous progeny we left behind us. But let us revert to the merry meeting previously alluded to. It is half-past two in the afternoon; we are gaily going through the figures of a country dance "speed the plough" perhaps, when the music stops short; every one is taken aback, and wonders at the cause of interruption. The arrival of two prelates, Bishop Plessis and Bishop Mountain, gave us the solution of the enigma; an aide-de-camp had mentioned to the bandmaster to stop, on noticing the entrance of the two high dignitaries of the respective churches. The dance was interrupted whilst they were there, and was resumed on their departure. Sir James had introduced this point of etiquette, from the respect he entertained for their persons.

"At three, the loud sound of a hunter's horn is heard in the distance;—all follow His Excellency, in a path cut through the then virgin forest of Powel Place. Some of the guests, from the length of the walk, began to think that Sir James had intended those who had not danced to take a "constitutional" before dinner, when, on rounding an angle, a huge table, canopied with green boughs, groaning under the weight of dishes, struck on their view—a grateful oasis in the desert. Monsieur Petit, the *chef de cuisine* has surpassed himself; like Vatel, I imagine he would have committed suicide had he failed to achieve the triumph, by which he intended to elicit our praise. Nothing could exceed in magnificence, in sumptuousness this repast—such was the opinion not only of the Canadians, for whom such displays were new, but also of the European guests, though there was a slight draw back to the perfect enjoyment of the dishes—*the materials which composed them we could not recognize*; so great was the artistic skill, so wonderful the manipulations of Monsieur Petit, the French cook.

"The Bishops left about half an hour after dinner, when dancing was resumed with an increasing ardor, but the cruel mammas were getting concerned respecting certain sentimental walks which their daughters were enjoying after sunset. They ordered them home, if not with that menacing attitude with which the goddess Calypso is said to have spoken to her nymphs, at least with frowns, so said the gay young *cavaliers*. By nine o'clock, all had re-entered Quebec."

sed, how many despatches settled, how many political points adjusted in the stormy days which saw the abolition of the Seigniorial Tenure and Clergy Reserves. At one of his brilliant postprandial speeches,—Lord Elgin was much happier at this style of oratory than his successor, Sir Edmund Head,—the noble Earl is reported to have said, alluding to Spencer Wood, "Not only would I willingly spend here the rest of my life, but after my death, I should like my bones to rest in this beautiful spot;" and still China and India had other scenes, other triumphs, and his Sovereign, other rewards for the successful statesman.

Sir Edmund Head's sojourn at Spencer Wood was marked by a grievous family bereavement; his only son, a promising youth of nineteen summers, was, in 1858, accidentally drowned in the St. Maurice, at Three Rivers, while bathing. This domestic affliction threw a pall over the remainder of the existence of His Excellency, already darkened by bodily disease. Seclusion and quiet were desirable to him.

A small private gate still exists at Spencer Grange, which at the request of the sorrowful father was opened through the adjoining property with the permision of the proprietor. Each week His Excellency, with his amiable lady, stealing a few moments from the burthen of affairs of State, would thus walk through unobserved to drop a silent tear, on the green grave at Mount Hermon, in which were entombed all the hopes of a noble house. On the 12th March, 1860, on a wintry evening, whilst the castle was a blaze of light and powdered footmen hurried through its sounding corridors, to relieve of their fur coats and mufflers, His Excellency's guests asked at a state dinner that night—Sir John A. Macdonald, Sir Geo. E. Cartier, Mr. Pennifather and others—the alarm of fire was sounded, and in a couple of hours, of the magnificent pile a few charred ruins only remained. There was no State dinner that night.

One of the last acts of the Ministry in retiring in 1861, was the signing of the contract to rebuild Spencer Wood. The appropriation was a very niggardly one, in view of the size of the structure required as a Vice-Regal residence. All meretricious ornaments in the design were of course left out. A square building, two hundred feet by fifty, was erected with the main entrance, in rear, on the site of the former lovely flower garden. The location of the entrance and consequent sacrifice of the flower garden for a court, left the river front of the dwelling for the private use of the inmates of the *Château* by excluding the public. Lord Monk, the new Governor General, took possession of the new Mansion and had a plantation of fir and other trees added to conceal the east end from public gaze. Many happy days were spent at Spencer Wood by His Lordship and family, whose private secretary, Denis Godly, Esq., occupied the picturesque cottage " Bagatelle,"* facing the Holland road, on the Spencer Grange property. If illustrious names on the Spencer Wood Visitor's Register could enhance the interest the place may possess, foremost, one might point to H. R. H. the Prince of Wales, visiting in 1860 the site probably more than once surveyed and admired, in 1791-4, by his grand-father, Prince Edward, Duke of Kent, in his drives round Quebec, with the fascinating Baroness de St. Laurent. Conspicuous amongst all those familiar with the portals of Spencer Wood, may be mention two other Royal Princes—the Duke of Edinburgh and Prince Arthur, Princess Louise ; with Dukes and Earls—the Duke of Newcastle, Manchester, Buckingham, Prince Napoléon, Generals Grant, Sherman, &c.

Since Confederation, Spencer Wood has been successively tenanted by Sir N. F. Belleau, Lieutenant-Governor Caron, Lieutenant-Governor Letellier de St. Just, and Lieutenant-Governor Robitaille, the present occupant of the seat.

---

* Now occupied by Hon. Chs. Hoare Ruthven, brother to Lord Ruthven and Capt. of the crack Sillery Corps, the 3rd Co. Quebec Garrison Artillery.

# MEMORABILIA.

Jacques Cartier landed on the banks of the Saint Charles..... Sept. 14, 1535

Quebec founded by Samuel de Champlain.................July 3, 1608

Fort St. Louis built at Quebec....................... 1620

Quebec surrendered to Admiral Kirk..................... 1629

Quebec returned to the French...................... 1632

Death of Champlain, the first Governor.................Dec. 25, 1635

Settlement formed at Sillery........................ 1637

A Royal Government formed at Quebec.................. 1663

Quebec unsuccessfully besieged by Admiral Phipps.......... 1690

Count de Frontenac died....................Nov. 28, 1698

Battle of the Plains of Abraham...............Sept. 13, 1759

Capitulation of Quebec....................Sept. 18, 1759

Battle of St. Foye—a French victory...............April 28, 1760

Canada ceded by treaty to England................... 1763

Blockade of Quebec by Generals Montgomery and Arnold.....Nov. 10, 1775

Death of Montgomery...................31st Dec., 1775

Retreat of Americans from Quebec...............May 6, 1776

Division of Canada into Upper and Lower Canada............. 1791

Insurrection in Canada........................ 1837

Second Insurrection......................... 1838

Union of the two Provinces in one................... 1840

Dominion of Canada formed...................July 1, 1867

Departure of English troops..................... 1870

Second Centenary of Foundation of Bishopric of Quebec by Monseigneur Laval........................Oct. 1st, 1674, 1874

Centenary of Repulse of Arnold and Montgomery before Quebec on 31st Dec., 1775...................31st Dec., 1875

Dufferin Plans of City embellishment, Christmas day.............. 1875

Departure of the Earl of Dufferin.............18th Oct., 1878

Arrival of the Marquis of Lorne and Princess Louise........4th June, 1879

www.ingramcontent.com/pod-product-compliance
Lightning Source LLC
Chambersburg PA
CBHW032240080426
42735CB00008B/934